ESCAPE PHILOSOPHY

Fig. 1. Detail from Hieronymus Bosch, *Ship of Fools* (1490–1500)

First published in 2022 by dead letter office, BABEL Working Group, an imprint of punctum books, Earth, Milky Way.
https://punctumbooks.com

The BABEL Working Group is a collective and desiring-assemblage of scholar-gypsies with no leaders or followers, no top and no bottom, and only a middle. BABEL roams and stalks the ruins of the post-historical university as a multiplicity, a pack, looking for other roaming packs with which to cohabit and build temporary shelters for intellectual vagabonds. BABEL is an experiment in ephemerality. Find us if you can.

ISBN-13: 978-1-68571-062-0 (print)
ISBN-13: 978-1-68571-063-7 (ePDF)

DOI: 10.53288/0416.1.00

LCCN: 2022940635
Library of Congress Cataloging Data is available from the Library of Congress

Interior design: Vincent W.J. van Gerven Oei
Cover design: Matthew Revert
Frontispiece: *Pandemonium! Magazine* 47, October 1996. Cover design by Matt Youngmark. With kind permission of the art director, J. Matthew Youngmark.

p. punctumbooks
spontaneous acts of scholarly combustion

HIC SVNT MONSTRA

Roy Christopher

Journeys Beyond the
Human Body

p.

Contents

PANDEMONIUM!
SCARY HALLOWEEN ISSUE!

#47 OCTOBER, 1996 FREE

GODFLESH

DOWNLOAD
GODHEADSILO
GIANTS CHAIR
KISS IT GOODBYE

Acknowledgments

When Godflesh's first full-length record came out on November 13, 1989, I was just out of high school. In an issue of SPIN *Magazine* at the time, Faith No More's Mike Patton described *Streetcleaner* as the sound of your Walkman's batteries running down. That was enough of an endorsement for me to seek out the record. As well versed as I was in the metal of the time, what I found was like nothing I'd ever heard.

So first, I have to thank Justin K. Broadrick. I first met Justin in late November of 1996 when Godflesh played Seattle on what was to be their last US tour until they reunited two decades later. I was the editor of *Pandemonium! Magazine,* Tacoma, Washington's own music monthly, which had just gone out of business, and I'd just put Godflesh on the cover of our final issue the month before.

I was on my way out the door for a job interview when the phone rang. It was the publicist at Earache Records, Godflesh's label at the time. She wanted to know if I knew anyone who could give the guys a ride to their in-store appearance at Cellophane Square in the U-district that afternoon before the show that night at the Fenix Underground. I distinctly remember my voice cracking as I said, "I could do that!"

All I was thinking during my interview was that I was going to pick up Godflesh right after. I couldn't remember the questions or my answers as I drove to their hotel in my 1983 Honda Civic hatchback. I was wearing a button-up shirt and a tie, and as Justin climbed into my tiny car he asked, "How was your interview?"

We spent that whole day together. He signed records for a line of fans, and we shopped for hip-hop CDs. Then we headed to the Fenix for soundcheck, dinner, and then the show. I didn't see Justin again until Jesu toured with Isis eleven years later in 2007. I was back in Seattle then. I took a bus up to Neumo's on Capitol Hill. As I was walking up the sidewalk on Pike, I spotted Justin hanging out the side door talking to two other dudes. When I approached, he said, "Hey, I know you — Roy!"

We've managed to stay in touch over all these years, through Godflesh, Jesu, Final, Godflesh again, and his countless other projects. It's because of Justin's art and friendship that this book exists, and he provided invaluable insight as I was writing it.

Many thanks to the early readers of this material, including Gary J. Shipley, Peter Bebergal, B.R. Yeager, Robert Guffey, Eugene Thacker, Aaron Weaver, Simon Sellars, Michael Schandorf, Scott Heim, Steven Shaviro, Rick Moody, Timothy Saccenti, Alex Burns, David Barker, Nicole Nesmith, and Claudia Dawson, for their insightful comments and kind words. Thanks to Mark Dery, whose 1996 book *Escape Velocity* is this one's namesake and should be considered one of its parents. Thanks to Chloë Manon at the Graveface Museum, Jeni Lambert at Earache Records, Mike Sullivan of Russian Circles, Trevor de Brauw of Pelican, Stephanie Marlow, Peter Beste, Reid Haithcock, Alap Momin, Will Brooks, Mike Manteca, Kim Coletta, Bill Barbot, John Mohr, Dominic Pettman, McKenzie Wark, Josh Gunn, Alyssa Byrkit, James Ward Byrkit, and Spike Jonze for their help with images, facts, and general encouragement. Thanks to Howard Rheingold, Erik Davis, and Shane Mauss for answering my drug questions. Thanks to Godflesh, Jawbox, Deafheaven, Wolves in the Throne Room, Celtic Frost, and Stalaggh for inspiration.

Michael Grasso deserves special mention for helping extensively during the editing process. Thanks also to Tariq Goddard, Josh Turner, and Johnny Bull at Repeater Books.

Thanks to Matthew Revert for another stellar cover design and for being collaborative and kind.

I was privileged once again to work with Vincent W.J. van Gerven Oei and Eileen A. Fradenburg Joy at punctum books. You should go subscribe and support their work at punctum now.

As always, thanks to my partner in all things, Lily Brewer. Her many thoughtful comments and insightful edits made this the book that it is. Our Love is God.

Remember:
You are immaculate.
You endure.
You persevere in a world of pure gravity and sound.
You are like light, like a sea of air.
You are history, and make all of history something else.

Every sound generated continues to vibrate into infinity.
Each sound you make then, every mutter, every scream,
*   every prayer,*
Added to the reverberations that never end.

Some sounds can change everything.

— John Duncan, *The Error*

me is a god, a god of sadness
exiled to this eternal hell
the people I helped, abandon me
I am denied what I want,
To love & to be happy
Being made a human
Without the possibility of BEING *human*
The cruelest of all punishments
To some I am crazy
It is so clear, yet so foggy
Everything's connected, separated
I am the only interpreter of this
Id rather have nothing than be nothing
Some say godliness isn't nothing
Humanity is the something I long for
I just want something I can never have
The story of my existence.

— Dylan Klebold, journal entry,
September 5, 1997.

Exit Tragedy

"Living: a body in search of a corpse."
— Eugene Thacker, *Infinite Resignation*[1]

"I think human consciousness is a tragic misstep in evolution. We became too self-aware. Nature created an aspect of nature separate from itself. We are creatures that should not exist by natural law. We are things that labor under the illusion of having a self, an accretion of sensory, experience and feeling, programmed with total assurance that we are each somebody, when in fact everybody is nobody. Maybe the honorable thing for our species to do is deny our programming, stop reproducing, walk hand in hand into extinction, one last midnight, brothers and sisters opting out of a raw deal."
— Rustin Cohle, *True Detective*[2]

"The wonder is not that people continue to create symbolic ritual systems, but that these systems go stale or become

---

1   Eugene Thacker, *Infinite Resignation* (London: Repeater Books, 2018), 128.
2   Nic Pizzolatto, *True Detective* (HBO, 2014).

perverted, and that people lose belief, often with anxiety, but also with a sense of liberation and relief."

— Charles Leslie[3]

We are all perpetually holding ourselves together. Our breath, our blood, our food, our spit, our shit, our thoughts, our attention — all tightly held, all the time. Then at death, we let it all out, oozing at once into the earth and gasping at last into the ether.

What if we let it slip before then? What if we were able to let ourselves loose and be as free as we can be? What if we got lost somewhere out there beyond ourselves? If it's all going down, why aren't we trying to push ourselves as far out as we can? If we try to hold ourselves together as we watch our world fall apart, we're holding ourselves back for nothing.

If this sounds like despair, it probably should. The more we realize about our place in the world, the worse that place seems to get. Much has been written about the mainstreaming of pessimism as a philosophy, thanks especially to Rustin Cohle (played by Matthew McConaughey) in season one of Nic Pizzolatto's *True Detective* television series. Echoes of Cohle's morose monologues, themselves echoes of the writings of Thomas Ligotti, Laird Barron, and E.M. Cioran, among others, can be found throughout this book.[4] Gary J. Shipley writes of the show, "the end has already happened, and all Rustin Cohle and Marty Hart [played by Woody Harrelson] can do is arrange the bodies in a pattern that makes them look less like bodies, more like things that might have existed in bodies, if those bodies

3   Charles Leslie, "Review of *The Ritual Process. Structure and Anti-Structure* by Victor W. Turner," *Science* 168, no. 3932 (May 1970): 704.

4   See Michael Calia, "Writer Nic Pizzolatto on Thomas Ligotti and the Weird Secrets of 'True Detective,'" *Wall Street Journal,* February 2, 2014, https://www.wsj.com/articles/BL-SEB-79577. Pizzolatto also mentions John Langan, Simon Strantzas, Robert W. Chambers, and Karl Edward Wagner, as well as Edgar Allan Poe and H.P. Lovecraft, among others.

hadn't been born human."[5] This resignation is evident not only in this show but many others, a malaise seeping into our minds through our media.

The second season of the show continues the gloom of the first. Though, as Ian Bogost points out, where Cohle got lost in his own head, the characters in season two get lost out in the world.[6] The physician and psychoanalyst Dr. John C. Lilly distinguished between what he called "insanity" and "outsanity." Insanity is "your life inside yourself"; outsanity is the chaos of the world, the cruelty of other people.[7] Dr. Lilly used isolation tanks and psychedelics to explore his mind, leaving his body behind. Sometimes we get lost in our heads. Sometimes we get lost in the world.

As the Earth sustains less and less life, and the life that is left is susceptible to more and more hostile viruses and disease, our physical forms are vulnerable. Growing up under the shadow of the Cold War, the end seemed far away, like a mushroom cloud in the distance. The apocalyptic rhetoric of Y2K, the direct attacks of 9/11, and the Mayan calendar collapse of 2012 all brought eschatology ever closer, to mindsets and media outlets everywhere. Given the hostility of the global climate and the polarity of the political climate, as well as the increasingly frequent mass shootings, it now feels like the end is lurking right outside the door, a killer with a knife at the ready. If we are to protect ourselves, we must move beyond our selves.

One of the many methods used in futures studies is called environmental scanning. "All futurists do environmental scanning," write Theodore J. Gordon and Jerome C. Glenn, "some

5 Gary J. Shipley, "Monster at the End: Pessimism's Locked Rooms and Impossible Crimes," in *True Detection,* eds. Edia Connole, Paul J. Ennis, and Nicola Masciandaro (London: Schism, 2014), 2.

6 "By contrast, S2 was pure collapse. Nothing mattered or had meaningful effect. Rust got lost in his head. Ray, Frank, Ani: in the world." @ibogost, *Twitter,* August 11, 2015.

7 See David Jay Brown, "From Here to Alterity and Beyond with John C. Lilly," in *Mavericks of the Mind: Conversations for the New Millennium,* eds. David Jay Brown and Rebecca McClen Novick (Berkeley: The Crossing Press, 1993), 206.

are more organized and systematic, all try to distinguish among what is constant, what changes, and what constantly changes."[8] The process, which includes several distant early warning techniques, from expert panels, literature reviews, internet searches, and conference monitoring, helps inform the pursuits of issues management and strategic planning. According to William Renfro, futurist and president of the Issues Management Association, issues management consists of four stages: identifying potential future issues, researching the background and potential impacts of these issues, evaluating issues competing for a corporation or nation's operations, and developing appropriate strategies for these operations.[9]

Science fiction stories and horror movies are other places we look to "see" the future. Simulations and speculations are much more fun and much safer than the real things. Spaceships, AI, robots, cyberspace, these all exist in some form in the real world, but the widespread perception of these contrivances comes from fiction. "In the context of sf," Adam Roberts writes, "this reification works most potently on the interconnected levels of representation of technology and the technologies of reproduction."[10] At varying levels, we look to science fiction and horror to show us the potential directions technology is going and the ways it will affect our lives. These speculative trajectories show us what's possible, even if it's just by showing us what's not.

The art critic Harold Rosenberg argued that the culture of any society is the debris of past cultures, that any current culture is the fallout of the former, more so than a cohesive system itself.[11] When we describe something as ahead of its time,

8   Jerome C. Glenn and Theodore J. Gordon, *Futures Research Methodology, V2.0* (Washington, DC: AC/UNU Millennium Project, 2003), 3.
9   William L. Renfro, *Issues Management in Strategic Planning* (Westport: Quorum Books, 1993), 67.
10 Adam Roberts, *Science Fiction: The New Critical Idiom* (New York: Routledge, 2006), 113. Roberts adds, "science as simulation is the reason why fictional science, or 'sf', is so much more fun to watch than real science."
11 See Victor Turner, *Dramas, Fields, and Metaphors: Symbolic Action in Human Society* (Ithaca: Cornell University Press, 1974), 14.

sometimes that means it took a long time to find an audience, but it could be that it was predicting a possible future. In what follows, we will explore scenarios that may not include living on this planet and some that may not include living at all. In order to explore the space after and beyond ourselves, we will employ ideas and artifacts from heavy metal music to science fiction and horror films: the dark debris of recent systems, the prescient, predictive, and prophetic pieces of the past. One possible escape is found in mechanized sound, starting with the heaviest metal of England.

Justin K. Broadrick's best-known band Godflesh emerged in the late 1980s from the cold concrete of Birmingham, the same oppressive environment that spawned metal pioneers Black Sabbath and Judas Priest. Godflesh's first full-length record, *Streetcleaner,* provides an apocalyptic soundtrack to the world from which it came. *Streetcleaner* plods along at the pace of some giant factory, guitars and bass pummeling to the sound of machines. The overall sound is simply crushing. With the creeping nihilism of nine tons of radioactive sludge, Godflesh grinds and growls through the flaws and floes of humanity. Chapter one establishes the sound of the end and launches us into the remaining themes of this book. Like Godflesh's music, this book is about the space beyond the bounds of the human body and the end of life itself.

Though the name "Godflesh" carries many connotations, one reading is that the body is all-powerful, a true master no matter the host. "The social body constrains the way the physical body is perceived," wrote the anthropologist Mary Douglas, "the physical experience of the body, always modified by the social categories through which it is known, sustains a particular view of society. There is a continual exchange of meanings between the two kinds of bodily experience so that each reinforces the categories of the other. As a result of this interaction the body itself is a highly restricted medium of expression."[12] Chapter two

---

12 Mary Douglas, *Natural Symbols: Explorations in Cosmology* (London: Barrie & Rockliff, 1970), 65. See also Mary Douglas, *Implicit Meanings: Essays*

delves into such definitions of the body, seeking a broad view, with a watchful eye for a way around these restrictions. Possible escape routes from our corporeal constraints include machines, rapture, drugs, and death. *Escape Philosophy* includes a chapter on each, concluding with a look at the end of our existence, a glimpse of a future without us.

Turbulent Bloodlines

As cyberculture became culture-at-large, the body anxieties of the original cyberpunks slowly seeped into the everyday. Often viewed as a threat to human livelihood, mechanization promises freedom from our frail bodies. Some imagine a very deliberate merging, postulating an uploading of human consciousness into the contrivances themselves. If we can build a better body and inhabit it instead of this one, why not? From the exosomatic augmentation of automobiles to the command-and-control of computers, chapter three explores the marriage of the human and the machine.

If we can't live here, perhaps there's somewhere else out there or some other form we might take. Maybe we'll get beamed up and away, saved from our own destruction by angels or aliens. "The shedding of our borrowed human bodies may be required in order to take up our new bodies belonging to the next world," read a Heaven's Gate poster from 1994. "If you want to leave with us, you must be willing to lose everything of this world in order to have life in the next. Cling to this world and you'll surely die."[13] In chapter four, we rise with the fallen and take flight with the chosen.

The cover image of Godflesh's debut album, *Streetcleaner,* is a shot from Ken Russell's 1980 movie *Altered States.* The film follows a scientist attempting to escape his body through his mind,

in *Anthropology* (London: Routledge & Keegan Paul, 1975).

13 See "The Shedding of Our Borrowed Human Bodies May Be Required in Order to Take Up Our New Bodies Belonging to the Next World," *HeavensGate.com,* August 18, 1994, https://heavensgate.com/book/611.htm.

using sensory-deprivation tanks and hallucinogens. It closely parallels the early work of sensory-deprivation and dolphin-intelligence researcher Dr. John C. Lilly. Exploring the extremes of neurophysiology, biophysics, and electronics, Lilly experimented on himself with isolation tanks and ketamine. In chapter five, we take a dose and blast off into inner space.

If life is not an option, then we can escape in death. Serial killers, school shooters, mass murderers, suicide bombers, terrorists, world leaders; if the flesh is their god, they are devoted to destroying it. The last resort of escape from the human body is to snuff out the consciousness inside. Eugene Thacker writes, "there are times when the stupidity of our species is so suffocating that even extinction will not suffice. Then I understand, if only briefly, the other motive for suicide: the need — the desperate need — to be rid of other people."[14]

So, finally, we're all doomed anyway. Wiping us from this world would relieve all of the tensions of the flesh and bring the ultimate, final brutality. Ghost hunting in a world spent spinning, chapter seven reads humanity its last rites and hangs around after we're gone, spectral spectators, as if we were able to fulfill the lifelong dream of attending our own funeral.[15]

Let us let go and light out for parts known and unknown, within and without. Let's escape our bodies, wandering and lost. If the only way out is through, then we're each already well on our way.

---

14 Thacker, *Infinite Resignation,* 183.
15 See David Leo Rice, "The Overlook Hotel," *The Believer,* October 31, 2017, https://believermag.com/logger/overlook/.

1

Godflesh
Compound Worlds

"We are going back to the future and forward to the past,
engaging all of history's villains and saints in quick time. […]
Ancient ethnic sores are belching fire while transnational
companies linked by satellites conduct their business oblivious
to the feudal past below."
— Don Beck and Christopher Cowan, *Spiral Dynamics*[1]

"Life on earth never settled down to do anything very good.
Science ran too far ahead of us too quickly, and the people
got lost in a mechanical wilderness, like children making over
pretty things, gadgets, helicopters, rockets; emphasizing the
wrong items, emphasizing machines instead of how to run the
machines. Wars got bigger and bigger and finally killed Earth."
— Ray Bradbury, *The Martian Chronicles*[2]

---

1   Don Beck and Christopher Cowan, *Spiral Dynamics: Mastering Values,
    Leadership, and Change* (New York: Wiley-Blackwell, 1996), 18.
2   Ray Bradbury, *The Martian Chronicles* (New York: Doubleday, 1950), 180.

> "I hope that when the world comes to an end, I can breathe a
> sigh of relief because there will be so much to look forward to."
> — Donnie Darko[3]

"It's just a matter of time, for me, before our ultimate extinction, and I can't say we don't deserve it."[4] This quotation from Justin K. Broadrick sums up his motivation as an artist. His prolific career involving countless bands and projects spans over three decades. But it also says a lot about what many would call his most important band and their most important record. That band is Godflesh, and that record is *Streetcleaner*. "I don't have a very optimistic view of humanity," Broadrick said in the early 1990s, not long after *Streetcleaner* had been unleashed on the world. "Eighty percent of it is shit, and as a whole, mankind is very weak and without any kind of purpose. Once in a while, people need to be crushed emotionally and intellectually to be reminded of reality. That's the basic purpose of our music."[5] Rebelling against their backgrounds and the very metal scene that spawned them, Broadrick says, "with Godflesh we were like, fuck everyone. And that was obviously cultivated even further to make an album like *Streetcleaner*."[6] Writer Simon Reynolds called it "a triumph in a void" at the time.[7]

In the late 1980s, metal was fast and heavy. The underground was ruled and regulated by thrash, death metal, and grindcore, each with its own set of stringent rules and rabid fans. Today's wildly popular black metal was still in its infancy. Godflesh's debut was sluggish in comparison, and they used a drum machine

---

3   Richard Kelly, dir., *Donnie Darko* (Newmarket, 2001).
4   Quoted in Luke Turner, "Greymachine: Justin Broadrick and Aaron Turner United," *The Quietus,* November 18, 2009, http://thequietus.com/articles/03246-greymachine-justin-broadrick-and-aaron-turner-united.
5   Quoted in René Walczak, "Godflesh: Strength Through Purity," *Propaganda* 19 (Fall 1992): 40–41.
6   Quoted in Anthony Bartkewitcz, "Vision: Escape: Justin Broadrick," *Decibel Magazine,* March 2007, 71.
7   Simon Reynolds, "Godflesh Streetcleaner," *Melody Maker,* October 14, 1989, 37.

instead of a live drummer, anathema in the stodgy metal underground. "For at least the first year that we played," Broadrick remembers, "there were people chanting, 'Where's the drummer?' or 'You're too fucking slow!'"[8] Their initial reception was not promising, but as Broadrick put it at the time, "it's got a sound, and it's unique. And it's fucking heavy."[9]

In sound and theme, Godflesh's *Streetcleaner* struggles with the limits of human abilities. After leaving his previous hardcore and grindcore bands behind, Broadrick had a vision for a new sound. As a huge hip-hop fan, he wanted to infuse and abuse the monolithic brutality of heavy metal with maniacal, neck-breaking beats no human could play. He enlisted the help of a drum machine, an Alesis HR-16, layering drum sounds into impossibly pummeling rhythms, rhythms no human drummer could maintain. It's the cruelty of all times, crushed together by a post-industrial machine. *Streetcleaner* is a genre-defying and a genre-defining record. In fact, the reunited Godflesh performed the record in its entirety at Holland's Roadburn Festival in 2011, illustrating its lasting influence. "It is an angsty record written by a couple of teenagers," he said of the performance, "and it still resonates now. In fact, even more so, to some extent."[10]

"Godflesh is totally borne from those first twenty-four years of my life that I spent in Birmingham," Broadrick remembers.[11] The bleak, industrial environs of Birmingham gave birth to other dark, canonically heavy outfits like Black Sabbath and Judas Priest. The oppression of being "amongst crowds of people, being surrounded by concrete," as he puts it, shaped who Broadrick is and the way he expresses it. "I don't think Godflesh would

---

8   Quoted in Bartkewitcz, "Vision: Escape," 71.
9   Quoted in Albert Mudrian, "Just Words from the Editor," *Decibel Magazine,* March 2007, 8.
10 Quoted in J.J. Koczan, "Jesu Interview: Justin Broadrick Confirms New Godflesh Studio Album, Discusses Jesu's Latest, Imperfection, Self-Indulgence, Roadburn, and Much More," *The Obelisk,* May 6, 2011, http://theobelisk.net/obelisk/2011/05/06/jesuinterview/.
11 Quoted in Roy Christopher, "Godflesh: Uneasy Listening," *Pandemonium! Magazine* 47 (October 1996): 22.

Fig. 1. A couple of teenagers: Benny Green and Justin K. Broadrick are Godflesh. Courtesy of Earache Records.

have existed if I'd come from another environment. It's absolutely a reflection of the environment that I grew up in."[12] Summing it up succinctly, J.J. Anselmi, author of *Doomed to Fail*, writes,

> Black Sabbath and Napalm Death reflect the negativity of industrial life, but Godflesh recreates the factory and its indifferent thrum. The band's self-titled album forces the brain down conveyer belts and through a maze of steel compactors that never seems to end, mirroring a life of toiling alongside machinery that could so easily grind your bones to dust.[13]

"With Godflesh, we try to aim at something quite off balance, off kilter, a lot different from anyone else,"[14] Broadrick told me in 1996. Since its inception, Godflesh has been Broadrick and Christian "Benny" Green with their drum machine, and as strange as it may seem for a band as heavy as Godflesh is, hip-hop has been an obvious element in their overall sound. "I think hip-hop is more important than any sort of rock music," states Broadrick matter-of-factly. "Most of the beats are fatter and heavier than your average rock n' roll riff."[15] One of the major sonic tenets of Godflesh is that under the monolithic basslines and ear-searing guitar riffs lie hip-hop's most brutal break beats. Not realizing what a total hip-hop head Justin is, people tend to miss the low-key references to the genre in Godflesh's music. Broadrick describes the collision and collusion of genres inherent in Godflesh's sound:

---

12 Quoted in Dimitri Nasrallah, "Justin Broadrick: Napalm Death – Godflesh – Techno Animal – Jesu – Pale Sketcher," *Exclaim!,* September 2010, http://exclaim.ca/Features/Timeline/JUSTIN_BROADRICK-Napalm_Death-Godflesh-Techno_Animal-Jesu-Pale_Sketcher.

13 J.J. Anselmi, *Doomed to Fail: The Incredibly Loud History of Doom, Sludge, and Post Metal* (Los Angeles: Rare Bird Books, 2020), 213.

14 Quoted in Christopher, "Godflesh: Uneasy Listening," 22.

15 Quoted in Roy Christopher, "Godflesh: Heads Ain't Ready," *SLAP Skateboard Magazine,* December 1997, 77.

I guess one of the things about metal is that it's really stigma-tised, even with myself in Godflesh, when we first became somewhat popular, I was very eager at that time to distance myself from metal, and I think that's because at the time there was very little like Godflesh. The most popular metal when Godflesh became popular in 1989/90 was the back-end of the hair metal thing, and Godflesh played with a lot of bands, a lot of tours in America like that, and I became quite repulsed by the whole circus of heavy metal. But, essentially, I've al-ways been excited by what's central to heavy metal, which is the sound, the texture of heavy metal. That was it, for me.[16]

To wit, the beat on the song "Christbait Rising" from *Street-cleaner* was Broadrick's attempt to copy the rhythm break from 1988's "Microphone Fiend" by Eric B. and Rakim. "We have our own bastardized idea of what we can do hip-hop-wise," he tells me. "It comes out even more perverted this way."[17]

In the early 1980s, photocopied fanzines and demo tapes were heavily circulating through underground networks via the postal service. Broadrick's interest in extreme music and in find-ing like-minded individuals naturally landed him in the middle of this subculture. He started his first band, Final, and record-ed many cassettes. Through these exchanges, he joined a band called Fall of Because. Benny Green, Paul Neville, and Diarmuid Dalton — all of whom Broadrick has worked with on different projects since — made up the rest of the band. Broadrick joined them on drums, replacing their drum machine. Fall of Because's one recorded demo, which was compiled with live clips and re-leased as the record *Life Is Easy* in 1999, hints at the cold nihil-ism that would become Godflesh's signature sound.

Broadrick had two more short stops before forming Godflesh proper: he played guitar on the first side of *Scum* (1986), the first

---

16 Quoted in Jonathan Horsley, "Justin Broadrick Interview: Godflesh, Grow-ing Up and Anarcho-punk," *Decibel Magazine,* October 7, 2011, http://www.decibelmagazine.com/featured/justin-broadrick-interview-godflesh-growing-up-and-anarcho-punk/.

17 Quoted in Christopher, "Heads Ain't Ready," 77.

record by grindcore pioneers Napalm Death, and drums for the down-tuned, sludgy, metal band Head of David. "Head of David already had an album out," Broadrick explains. "They were the only people I knew who had fans and actually had a record in the shops. It wasn't just opportunistic for me, that first Head of David album I actually adored. I thought it was fucking amazing. With Napalm Death, we played with them a few times, and they were absolutely stunning. When their drummer left, they saw me drum with Fall of Because and invited me to join."[18]

His exit from Head of David was the real beginning of Godflesh. "They wanted to lose a lot of the noise and the qualities that had attracted me to that band," he says. "So, when they kicked me out of the band, I thought, right, I want to do something that takes the basic premise of where I wanted to go with Head of David, low-tune everything, make it brutal,"[19] to take it "to the gutter, make it more machine-like."[20] In the meantime, Fall of Because had broken up, leaving Benny Green free to join Broadrick's new project. "Godflesh really became my vision, and Ben Green was really into the same type of stuff [...] and we already had our songs from Fall of Because so we began with those. [...] I was really influenced by people using drum machines, most notably some of the hip-hop at the time: Public Enemy, Eric B & Rakim. When I first heard some of those records, I was astonished at the brutality of their drum machines, and I really was excited by that sound. I really wanted something inhuman sounding and beyond human capability. And I was already a drummer, so I knew what beats I wanted to hear. I wanted to hear them in the most disgusting, heavy fashion going."[21] Their self-titled debut EP on Swordfish Records made the promises that 1989's *Streetcleaner* finally delivered on: songs awash in wailing, scraping guitars, dirge-like, lumbering bass

18 Quoted in Nasrallah, "Justin Broadrick."
19 Ibid.
20 Quoted in Bartkewitcz, "Vision: Escape."
21 Quoted in Nasrallah, "Justin Broadrick."

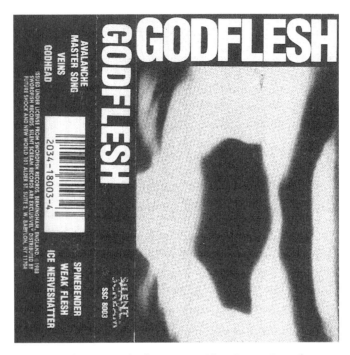

Fig. 2. Primal promises: the first cassette. Silent Scream Records, 1988.

lines, brutal, machine-driven beats, and Broadrick's anguished vocals. It was visceral and like nothing else at the time.

The second wave of industrial music, a beat-driven and mechanistic subgenre that found its roots in Throbbing Gristle, Einstürzende Neubauten, and Lou Reed's *Metal Machine Music,* was in full swing. Though no one else was mixing metal with machines quite like Godflesh, fueled by the popularity of Ministry, Skinny Puppy, Nine Inch Nails, and the output of Chicago's WaxTrax Records, the movement gave audiences a cultural reference point and made *Streetcleaner* an underground hit for Godflesh and their label Earache Records. It wasn't long before major labels came courting.

"I remember being stunned when I heard that first Korn album," Broadrick said in 2007, "because there's so much Godflesh in that, but used in this commercial way. It was weird. Like, wow, I guess it had to happen at some point; somebody had to take these sorts of sounds and make them digestible."[22] The full reach of *Streetcleaner*'s influence is difficult to gauge, but it's safe to say that much of what is considered metal in the twenty-first century wouldn't exist without it. Godflesh has always pushed limits in one direction or another. *Streetcleaner* is the germinal industrial-metal hybrid sound that bands all over the world are still trying to recreate, but Godflesh continued innovating. Since officially disbanding Godflesh in 2002, Broadrick has been busy with a band called Jesu, whom he named after the last song on the last Godflesh record, *Hymns* (2001), indicating a continuation of sorts of their spirit if not sound, and his original musical outlet Final, among other various remixes and collaborations. With the reuniting of Godflesh in 2010, Broadrick admits that he finds himself at home in the band. "I think Godflesh is still presenting exactly what I grew up with and exactly what runs through my blood," he said in 2011. "It's really important that that sense of expression is back in my life. I think I'd lost it through Jesu. But really, it's not just some re-visitation for me, it really feels like I've gone back to what I am in a way."[23]

"*Streetcleaner* was mostly culled from my teenage years," Justin Broadrick tells me more recently, "so there's a lot of the pain of transitioning from a child to a teenager, and my inability to come to terms with being an adult, and what the adult world brings: the pain of love, the pain of responsibility, etc."[24] The noisy machine that cleans pavement notwithstanding, the connotations of the name *Streetcleaner* are numerous, and Broadrick has referenced many of them over the years. "I change my angle on it often," he says, "chiefly due to 'maturing.'"[25] It's also street slang for an Uzi submachine gun.

---

22 Quoted in Bartkewitcz, "Vision: Escape."
23 Ibid.
24 Email with the author, February 16, 2021.
25 Ibid.

"I found it terrifying but also ambiguous and as a consequence very powerful," Broadrick tells me. "I wanted to revel
in the fear of almost everything I experienced as a kid, grasp
it, and attempt to become empowered by it, hence making a
bloated, filthy, primitive punk-like expression of the term."[26] As
we unpack the themes evident in Godflesh's music in what follows, the connotations and coincidences pile up pretty quickly.

---

26 Ibid.

2

Body
The Root of All People

"I wish I could peel away your humid, human skin
And attach you to me, parasitically."
— Milemarker, "Insect Incest"[1]

"The body, like most things, is a tool. The body's morality
depends on its user. The body's morality is determined by the
types and amounts of consumption it participates in. The body
is a filter. The body is a filter for language. The body is a filter
for reality, which it distills into image. The body filters image.
The body is an image. The body is image."
— Elle Nash, *Nudes*[2]

"The heart is a rotten root twining
Through soil feasting on droplets."
— George L. Clarke, *Westlake*[3]

---

1   Milemarker, "Insect Incest," on *Sex Jams* [7" single] (New Gretna: Blood-link Records, 1999).
2   Elle Nash, *Nudes* (Ann Arbor: Short Flight/Long Drive Books, 2020), 148.
3   George L. Clarke, *Westlake and Selected Writings* (Los Angeles: Sargent House, 2017), n.p.

It's not like it looks on TV. You never see the open torso of a body heaving and sucking after a bullet, a piece of shrapnel, or a chunk of flying concrete has ripped right through it. The worst part is the smell: somewhere between bad breath and warm shit. And it's inescapable. If the blood and guts get to be too much, you can look away. You can't get way from the smell.

Bodies are gross. Getting out of them remains one of the most pervasive and persistent human fantasies. Fragile and frail, they fail us. They suffer injuries. They decay. From feeling the limits of this sluggish shell to seeing it as a prison cell, everyone is looking for a way out.

Remove This Shell

Regularly referencing the limits of humanity in general and of the human body specifically, the lyrics on Godflesh's *Street-cleaner* include laconic lines like, "you breed, like rats," "bleed dry mankind," "remove this shell," "life / Our life / My life / Is expendable," "There has to be someone killed," "hell / Is where I lie / Now take the power / When we all die / We all die," and "the world shall shed / A tiny tear."[4] Death and extinction appear throughout. It might sound like typical heavy metal fare, but Broadrick bristles at the connotation.

"I've always hated metal," he tells me.

I've just used and abused it. I think people like to think that before we made *Streetcleaner* that we were some long-hair band who'd just discovered industrial music when that's not the case at all. The first music I was into was punk rock. It's so hard to convey these ideas to these people. They always come to me with how metal should go back to what it was in the eighties, and I'm like, "bloody hell!" I've always found metal rather conservative.[5]

---

4   Godflesh, *Streetcleaner* [LP] (London: Earache Records, 1989).
5   Quoted in Roy Christopher, "Heads Ain't Ready," SLAP *Skateboard Magazine,* December 1997.

Fig. 3. Faces of the 'Flesh: Justin Broadrick and Benny Green. Courtesy of Earache Records.

Godflesh has not only always rebelled against the strict confines of genre distinctions, but they never really fit them anyway. *Streetcleaner* grinds and growls like a flailing, failing factory: claustrophobic, misanthropic, foreboding, and forbidding yet dead deliberate in every aspect. "This was the antithesis of the old archaic image of cartoon, all conquering, always male, metal," Broadrick says in 2022. "And I've always felt the absolute opposite. If I want to hurt anyone, it's myself, for a start. And I feel like if it's the enemy of anything, Godflesh was always just the enemy of ignorance in all its forms."[6]

Justin Broadrick was born on August 15, 1969 in Birmingham, an "unpleasant" area that he describes as "the Detroit of England."[7] His first few years were spent on an actual hippie commune. Then he, his mom, and stepfather — his biologi-

---

6   Quoted in Antonio Poscic, "Out Demons Out," *The Wire,* April 2022, 30.
7   Quoted in Dimitri Nasrallah, "Justin Broadrick: Napalm Death – Godflesh – Techno Animal – Jesu – Pale Sketcher," *Exclaim!,* September 2010, http://exclaim.ca/Features/Timeline/JUSTIN_BROADRICK-Napalm_Death-Godflesh-Techno_Animal-Jesu-Pale_Sketcher.

cal father was a heroin addict whom he didn't see until he was 15-years old — moved into a council estate, the public housing projects of England. By the age of 12, Broadrick found punk rock like Crass, industrial bands like Throbbing Gristle and Whitehouse, and Krautrock like Can, as well as Brian Eno's early ambient work, all of which would inform his own musical output. He started messing around with some of his stepfather's music gear and taught himself guitar. "[W]hen I began to play guitar," he explains,

> I mastered one bar chord and realized that I could play any Crass song I wanted. That was pretty satisfying in itself. "Music" was like a dirty word when I went to school in 1978. Everyone was just into football hooliganism. But at home, I was absolutely inspired at a very young age to act in my environment, both in the form of music and, to some extent, against the oppressive environment I was in."[8]

Finding oneself trapped in a body can be a traumatic experience. When that body is walled-in by a city with cement and a family fraught with addiction, escape is high priority. When that body is left all alone, isolated from all other bodies, escape is high priority.

In the meantime, we put a lot on them. Bodies provide us with the illusion of permanence. For some of us, the body is a canvas, here to display the trials and traumas of the mind. We tattoo them with the symbols and sigils of our life's stories, its highs and lows that we don't want to forget. Our bodies display the scars of jumps and falls, attempts and fails. For others, the body is merely a vessel to carry them through this life, a physical manifestation of a time on this planet. Either way, we adorn them, embellish them, cover them, uncover them, care

---

8   Joseph Burnett, "Extreme Language: An Interview with Justin K. Broadrick," *The Quietus,* May 9, 2012, http://thequietus.com/articles/08733-jk-flesh-interview-justin-broadrick.

for them, curse them, protect them, mutilate them, use them, abuse them, augment them, extend them.

Boundary Trouble

Once declaring that an individual is a "montage of loosely as-sembled parts," and furthermore that when "you are on the phone or on the air you have no body,"[9] Marshall McLuhan's brand of media theory dismembered the body. The music and media we make, as well as the machines we use to make them are all extensions of ourselves in McLuhan's terms, but they're also prosthetics, amputating parts of ourselves as they extend them, turning us into cyborgs. Judith Butler reassembles the body as "culturally intelligible";[10] that is, as one that is recognized by the members of its society, what Sandy Stone calls the "legible body."[11] On the phone, on the air, or online, you are "read" as a member. Stone also postulates the "illegible body" that exists "quantumlike in multiple states": "their social system includes other people, quasi people or delegated agencies that represent specific individuals, and quasi agents that represent 'intelligent' machines, clusters of people, or both."[12] This discourse doesn't just fragment the body into gendered, sexualized, augmented, and virtual codes and constructs, but also addresses the fact that concerns about the body haven't been marginalized by tech-nological evolution as largely predicted. Just as telecommut-ing de-emphasizes place in that we can work from anywhere, it reemphasizes it in that where we are matters more. Not having a body or having a technologically mediated one now matters in a different way.

9   Marshall McLuhan, *The Gutenberg Galaxy: The Making of Typographic Man* (Toronto: University of Toronto Press, 1962), xxix.
10 Judith Butler, *Gender Trouble: Feminism and the Subversion of Identity* (New York: Routledge, 1990), 167.
11 Allucquère Rosanne (Sandy) Stone, "Will the Real Body Please Stand Up?" in *Reading Digital Culture,* ed. David Trend (Malden: Blackwell, 2001), 195.
12 Ibid., 196.

Even from a steadfastly feminist stance, we tend to focus on the narratives and discourses surrounding issues of the body more so than their material systems and conditions. As Donna Haraway, the author of "The Cyborg Manifesto," puts it, "the cyborg is a kind of disassembled and reassembled, postmodern collective and personal self."[13] N. Katherine Hayles adds that cyborgs are "simultaneously entities and metaphors, living beings, and narrative constructions."[14] In such a muddled milieu, the power lies in the control of these analogies and their boundaries. Without the philosophical consideration and creative expression that art provides us, trying to conceive of a self beyond the body is pointless.

Another term for the feminist in Haraway's work is the posthuman, and philosopher Rosi Braidotti pushes the analogies and boundaries of the body past postmodernity in her 2013 book, *The Posthuman.* Cybernetics defined humans as "information-processing systems whose boundaries are determined by the flow of information."[15] Braidotti pays special attention to these flows, building from three areas of thought: moral philosophy, science and technology, and anti-humanist philosophies of subjectivity. Paul Virilio shortened the term "cyberspace" from its imaginary, original form "cybernetic space-time,"[16]

---

13 Donna J. Haraway, *Simians, Cyborgs, and Women: The Reinvention of Nature* (New York: Routledge, 1990), 163.

14 N. Katherine Hayles, *How We Became Posthuman: Virtual Bodies in Cybernetics, Literature, and Informatics* (Chicago: University of Chicago Press, 1999), 114.

15 Ibid., 114. Hayles adds, "when system boundaries are defined by information flows and feedback loops rather than epidermal surfaces, the subject becomes a system to be assembled and disassembled rather than an entity whose organic wholeness can be assumed" (160).

16 Paul Virilio, *The Art of the Motor,* trans. Julie Rose (Minneapolis: University of Minnesota Press, 1995), 140. Bradotti writes, "in the perspective of French Post-structuralism, the human organic mass, the body, is the first manufacturer of technology in that it seeks for organic extension of itself first through tools, weapons, and artifacts, then through language, the ultimate prosthesis." Rosi Braidotti, *Nomadic Subjects: Embodiment and Sexual Difference in Contemporary Feminist Theory* (New York: Columbia University Press, 1994), 44.

which evokes the ultimate mechanical prosthesis of the mind, a planet-spanning, command-control system to end all such systems. Even now, a globalized network culture decentralizes the humanist subject's stability in space and time. The upending of anthropocentrism upsets the hierarchy of the species, and the technological mediation of the human subject disrupts our ideas about bodily norms.

The body's boundaries are permeable. Not so permanent after all, in the long tail of gender, the body's own physical signifiers are less important than how we feel within them. Moving beyond the body as we know it means subverting any extant grand narrative or theory of the embodied human and any attempt at a new one. It means rejecting the demonization of science and technology. It means embracing the nonlinearity of our posthuman times, the further fragmentation of our selves, and the permeability of our bodily boundaries and definitions. Haraway writes, "it means both building and destroying machines, identities, relationships."[17] It means rethinking the lines we've drawn through the ones we've crossed.[18]

Any attempt to escape the body only reifies its limits. Every augmentation brings its own detriment. Every route out has its own pitfalls.[19]

This Is the Voice[20]

The tagline to the 2009 movie *Moon* reads, "250,000 miles from home, the hardest thing to face… is yourself." *Moon* tells the story of astronaut Sam Bell, who on his last two weeks of a three-year solitary contract harvesting Helium 3 from the far side of

17 Haraway, *Simians, Cyborgs, and Women,* 181.
18 See Brian Rotman, *Becoming Beside Ourselves: The Alphabet, Ghosts, and Distributed Human Being* (Durham: Duke University Press, 2008).
19 As Shipley puts it, "it is for this reason that the way out is always nothing, always negative, always elusive and void: God, reality, death, ourselves." Gary J. Shipley, *Stratagem of the Corpse: Dying with Baudrillard, a Study of Sickness and Simulacra* (London: Anthem Press, 2020), 34.
20 Agent Orange, *This Is the Voice* [LP] (Los Angeles: Enigma Records, 1986).

Fig. 4. Sam I am: Sam Rockwell as Sam Bell in *Moon,* 2009. Licensed by Alamy.

the Moon, out of sight of Earth. During his last two weeks of his lunar stay, the daily routine of his mission starts to devolve into madness and second-guessing. Sam is haunted by hallucinations of a teenage girl and an older man. Overwhelmed, he chants "two more weeks, two more weeks" like a mantra.

Even though his existence on the Moon is largely attended to by communication media and technology, Sam can't escape himself. He is alone aside from his computerized companion, and the messages he sends to and receives from earth are prerecorded, unbeknownst to him. Even in its celestial setting, *Moon* is more concerned with inner space than outer space. Writer and director Duncan Jones wrote the role of Sam Bell specifically for Sam Rockwell, and his having the same first name is no accident. Jones explains, "one of the reasons why I left the name Sam is I wanted [Rockwell] to have that feeling of it being a little uncomfortable, that he's having to face himself, because in the story, that's what happens."[21]

Now, is the fissure caused by the Mother, the Father, or the Other? In *Moon,* there's more than one Sam. Actually, there are more than two Sams. Judith Butler asks, "what if there is an Other who does violence to another Other?"[22] What we think is the original Sam on the Moon eventually encounters two other Sams, and two of them find a store of endless Sams. Aching to resolve his existential identity crisis, the Sam we've followed from the beginning calls his wife on Earth. His daughter, Eve, answers the videophone, and explains that his wife died years before. During their brief conversation, he hears his own voice from off screen. This opens the real fissure. Recognizing the sound of his own voice after a moment of detachment, Sam immediately hangs up. The words spoken from Earth do not matter; only the voice with which they are spoken. Seeing himself in the flesh on the Moon was one kind of encounter. Hearing himself speak from Earth was more than he could take. Butler writes, "we cannot, under contemporary representation, hear the agonized cry or be compelled or commanded by the face."[23] Only the voice can do this. The voice is the presence of the real.

The voice without language is the seat of suffering.[24] Like machine parts pushed past their limits, cogs stripped bare of their

---

21 Quoted in Marjorie Baumgarten, "Sitting in a Tin Can, Where Hell Is Still Other People: Director Duncan Jones on His Debut Film, 'Moon'," *The Chronicle,* July 10, 2009, https://www.austinchronicle.com/screens/2009-07-10/808103/

22 Butler, *Gender Trouble,* 139.

23 Ibid., 150. Steve Connor adds, "the voice may be grasped as the mediation between the phenomenological body and its social and cultural contexts." Steven Connor, *Dumbstruck: A Cultural History of Ventriloquism* (Oxford: Oxford University Press, 2000), 12.

24 Rotman writes, "the affect proper to human speech, which pertains to moods, feelings, passions, attitudes, or emotions it conveys and induces, lies in its tone, a phenomenon determined by the gestures of the voice, those auditory movements of the body within utterance: its hesitations, silences, emphases, sharpness, timbre, musicality, changes of pitch, and other elements of prosody. The alphabet knows nothing of all this. It eliminates tone and any kind of prosody completely: it reduces the voice to

teeth, language lost to pain brings us back to the body. When Sam hears the sound of his own voice on the line to earth, he is returned to himself. Witness Broadrick's howls or the shrieks and shrills of other metal vocalists. In these extreme musical forms, the voice is employed as another instrument or texture. Mladen Dolar writes, "as soon as it departs from its textual anchorage, the voice becomes senseless and threatening."[25] Moreover, when technology tethers the voice with language through text or some other media, we are aware of the Other and sometimes our own Other. We do not like to realize ourselves as Other. We do not like to realize the humanity of the Other. These realizations are nowhere more present than in the voice. Seeing is one thing. There remains a distance to the visual. Hearing is in your head. Dolar challenges the primacy of the visual by positioning the voice as "the first manifestation of life."[26] That is, before the image of the mirror, before self-recognition via the gaze, it is through our voices and our media that we realize that we are, and that we are Other. Dolar adds, "the voice is both the subtlest and most perfidious form of the flesh."[27] The voice of pain or the voice of the Other gets right inside you.

Sound mind, sound body: the body is inescapable, even if only in sound.

---

words and writes 'what's said' but not the manner of its saying, its delivery, how what's said is said. What, one can ask, would be the features of a 'speaker': and the affect of a 'voice' known only through alphabetic writing?" Rotman, *Becoming Beside Ourselves,* xxxiii.

25 Mladen Dolar, *A Voice and Nothing More* (Cambridge: MIT Press, 2006), 43.

26 Ibid., 39.

27 Ibid., 48.

3

Machine

Mechanical Reproduction

"Nothing of us will survive. We will be killed not by the gun but by the glad-hand. We will be destroyed not by the rocket but by the automobile…"

— Ettil in Ray Bradbury, "The Concrete Mixer"[1]

"It is clear that the car crash is seen as a fertilizing rather than a destructive experience, a liberation of sexual and machine libido, mediating the sexuality of those who have died with an erotic intensity impossible in any other form."

— J.G. Ballard, *Atrocity Exhibition*[2]

"The lost and found are incalculable."

— Fred Moten, *Black and Blur*[3]

I ordered the seven-inch of Jawbox's 1993 single "Motorist" as soon as I knew it was available. The lyrics, even for a Jawbox song, were striking. "Accidental, maybe," ponders J. Robbins,

1   Ray Bradbury, *The Illustrated Man* (New York: Doubleday, 1951), 225.
2   J.G. Ballard, *The Atrocity Exhibition* (London: Jonathan Cape, 1970), 157.
3   Fred Moten, *Black and Blur: Consent Not to Be a Single Being* (Durham: Duke University Press, 2017), xvii.

"restraints too frayed to withhold me."[4] Paul Virilio once wrote that whenever we invent a new technology, we also invent a new kind of accident.[5] We might never again invent a technology that is so prone to accidents as we have with the automobile. Hearing Jawbox play that song live again reminded me of the wreckage of artifacts piled up in my head around it.

Over Zach Borocas's lurching beat, Kim Coletta's chugging bass, and his and Bill Barbot's dual, dueling guitar feedback, Robbins yells, "when you examined the wreck, what did you see? Glass everywhere and wheels still spinning free."[6] I remember immediately thinking of the 1973 Ballard novel, *Crash*. In the simplest of terms, *Crash* is about a group of people who fetishize car crashes. Most of them have been in actual accidents, but they also stage their own. They are sexually aroused by the impact as well as the aftermath, the energies and the injuries.

Though I hadn't read it at the time, I thought Robbins had. I found out recently that the song is actually about a car accident that happened in Chicago while Jawbox was on tour. While back in town during the last night of the band's 2019 summer reunion tour, Robbins told the story on stage at the Metro. In light of this new information, I've tried to rewire my interpretation of the song. In my head Jawbox's "Motorist" remains connected to Ballard's *Crash*.

Compare Robbins's singing, "cracked gauges carry messages for me. Calls and responses you can't see"[7] to Ballard writing, "in front of me the instrument panel had been buckled inwards, cracking the clock and speedometer dials. Sitting here in this deformed cabin, filled with dust and damp carpeting, I tried to visualize myself at the moment of collision, the failure of the technical relationship between my own body, the assumptions

---

4   J. Robbins, "Motorist," on *Jackpot Plus* [7" single], recorded by Jawbox (Washington, DC: Dischord Records, 1993).

5   Paul Virilio, "The Museum of Accidents," trans. Chris Turner, *International Journal of Baudrillard Studies* 3, no. 2 (2006), https://baudrillardstudies. ubishops.ca/the-museum-of-accidents/.

6   Robbins, "Motorist."

7   Ibid.

of the skin, and the engineering structure which supported it";[8] or "the wounds on my knees and chest were beacons tuned to a series of beckoning transmitters, carrying the signals, unknown to myself, which would unlock this immense stasis and free these drivers for the real destinations set for their vehicles, the paradises of the electric highway."[9] This motorized mysticism, the idea that technology enables and endures unintended uses and conjures and communicates unintended messages runs parallel to the cult of the car. Scriptures superimposed on the roads. Messages, transmitters, signals, all performing a discourse of dread, a dialogue of deadly trauma.

Automobile-accident numbers are routinely trotted out in comparison to whatever disaster is threatening human lives at the time. Gun violence, viral plagues, and various cancers are all measured at least annually against the deaths we inflict driving these vehicles. As Zadie Smith writes in *The Guardian,* quoting Ballard himself, "like the characters in *Crash* we are willing participants in what Ballard called 'a pandemic cataclysm that kills hundreds of thousands of people each year and injures millions.' The death-drive, Thanatos, is not what drivers secretly feel, it's what driving explicitly *is*."[10] When we hear the statistics, we might worry for a second, noting those we know who've passed away on the road or been maimed by molded metal, but we soon continue our car-enabled commutes undeterred, autocide awaiting.[11]

Death isn't the only Freudian trope that these stories stir up. Sex is wound into the car accident as well, both as pornography and as intimacy. "When Ballard called *Crash* the first 'pornographic novel about technology,'" Smith continues, "he referred not only to a certain kind of content but to pornography as an

---

8   J.G. Ballard, *Crash: A Novel* (London: Jonathan Cape, 1973), 68.

9   Ibid., 44.

10 Zadie Smith, "Sex and Wheels: Zadie Smith on J.G. Ballard's 'Crash,'" *The Guardian,* July 4, 2014, https://www.theguardian.com/books/2014/jul/04/zadie-smith-jg-ballard-crash.

11 I lifted the word "autocide" from Anthony Smith, *The Body* (New York: Walker & Company, 1968), 306.

Fig. 5. Eros on the Highway. Image by the author.

organizing principle."[12] Pornography is itself a form of media that stimulates the body. We might not enjoy it or admit that we do, but we all understand it as a concept. Its meaning is not a mystery. In *Crash*, it acts as a skewed skeuomorph. As Ballard writes, it is "as if the presence of the car mediated an element which alone made sense of the sexual act."[13] And aren't cars always already sexualized? The metaphor is close at hand, as visceral as it is vehicular: pistons and spark plugs, revving and thrusting, hands gripping curves and contours galore.

The jutting juxtaposition of body parts and auto parts and the blending of bodily fluids and engine oils might be more disturbing when thought of as intimacy than as pornography. In Julia Ducournau's *Titane* (2021), the shock of Alexia (played by Agathe Rousselle) having intercourse with automobiles quickly fades. What lingers are the moments when she is simply affectionate toward them, hugging or caressing their cold, metal ex-

---

12   Smith, "Sex and Wheels."
13   Ballard, *Crash*, xii.

teriors. "The real shock of *Crash* is not that people have sex in or near cars," Smith writes, "but that technology has entered into even our most intimate human relations."[14] It's not the violence of the sex act but the intimate presence of technology there that chafes our sensibilities.[15] It's not the sexual appropriation of a mechanical contrivance but the emotional possibility of love that bothers us. "Traditional warnings against the evils of mediation reach an ironic zenith in this portrait of 'the most terrifying casualty of the century: the death of affect,'"[16] Dominic Pettman notes grimly. With sex and technology crammed together in this context, we can't decide if it's better or worse to care.

No matter how you feel about them, car crashes and sexual encounters force one thing on everyone: exposure. From fender benders to total immobility, no one wants to get caught in the act, caught with their pants down, *in flagrante delicto.* Ballard himself described *Crash* as a forced look in the mirror.[17] "You can see your reflection in the luminescent dash," Daniel Miller sings on The Normal's *Crash*-inspired track, "Warm Leatherette."[18] "Seduced reflection in the chrome," Siouxsie Sioux adds on the Creatures' Ballardian "Miss the Girl."[19] "New way to see what's laid plain in front of me," Robbins wails on "Motorist." "Noth-

---

14 Smith, "Sex and Wheels."

15 For examples regarding David Cronenberg's 1996 film adaptation, see Martin Barker, Jane Arthors, and Ramaswami Harindranath, *The Crash Controversy: Censorship Campaigns and Film Reception* (London: Wallflower Press, 2001).

16 Dominic Pettman, *After the Orgy: Toward a Politics of Exhaustion* (Albany: SUNY Press, 2002), 80. Pettman is quoting V. Vale and Andrea Juno, eds., *RE/Search #8/9: J.G. Ballard* (San Francisco: Re/Search Publications, 1984).

17 Quoted in Peter Bradshaw et al., "How J.G. Ballard Cast His Shadow Right Across the Arts," *The Guardian,* April 20, 2009, https://www.theguardian.com/books/2009/apr/20/jg-ballard-film-music-architecture-tv. They themselves quote a sample of Ballard speaking from the Manic Street Preachers song "Mausoleum," on *The Holy Bible* [LP] (New York: Epic Records, 1984).

18 Daniel Miller, "T.V.O.D.," on *Warm Leatherette* [7" single], recorded by The Normal (London: Mute Records, 1978).

19 Siouxsie Sioux & Budgie, "Miss the Girl," on *Feast* [LP], recorded by The Creatures (London: Polydor, 1983).

ing better than a look at what I shouldn't see."[20] The car accident seen as porn, a form we can't look away from.

No one wants to get caught with their body thrown clear at odd angles, the contents of their car strewn, the whole of their very lives lying limp on the pavement. Every illicit tryst implies its own exit strategy. On "Motorist," Robbins concludes, "turn your back, just drive on past, because nothing is better than getting out fast."

Look hard and then look away. The fastest car is the getaway.

Uncanny Cartographies

It's been over a decade. A decade without J.G. Ballard. It should be more noticeable. Like filling an empty pool with emptiness, to paraphrase China Miéville.[21] A void of perspective, crumbling and gaping at our heels. Everyone should feel it. It goes without saying, but I'll say it anyway: this is the way, step inside.

His work has been translated to the screen by directors with styles as varied as Steven Spielberg (*Empire of the Sun,* 1987) and David Cronenberg (*Crash,* 1996). He was interviewed by countless talented writers, including Jon Savage, V. Vale, Will Self, Richard Kadrey, John Gray, Simon Sellars, and Mark Dery. His influence is found in sound from Joy Division, The Jesus and Mary Chain, Sisters of Mercy, K.K. Null, and Gary Numan to Madonna, Radiohead, Trevor Horn, Cadence Weapon, and Danny Brown, as well as the aforementioned Creatures and The Normal. His writing and thinking are broad enough to elude categories and focused enough to remain absolutely singular. His work gerrymanders categorical distinctions, defining and defying its own boundaries as it goes. I think of him in the same way I think of Octavia E. Butler, Ray Bradbury, Thomas Pynchon, Don DeLillo, and Samuel R. Delany — as giants beyond genre.

---

20 Robbins, "Motorist."
21 China Miéville, "Introduction," in J.G. Ballard, *Miracles of Life: Shanghai to Shepperton, an Autobiography* (New York: Liveright, 2008), ix–xiv.

"I suppose we are moving into a realm where inner space is no longer just inside our skulls but is in the terrain we see around us in everyday life," Ballard said in 1974; "we are moving into a world where the elements of fiction are that world — and by fiction I mean anything invented to serve imaginative ends, whether it is invented by an advertising agency, a politician, an airline, or what have you. These elements have now crowded out the old-fashioned elements of reality."[22] Since then, a lot of mental offloading and cognitive outsourcing has occurred, our inner thoughts texture-mapped onto every surface. In that meantime some of Ballard's children have emerged in mongrel forms and curtained corners of mass media. Think *Wild Palms* or *Jackass* or the ever-blurring lines between reality and show, news and entertainment. "It's not news," Ballard wrote, "it's entertainment news. A documentary on brain surgery is about entertainment brain surgery." Inversely, Ballard collaged and kludged together the sets of his own *Atrocity Exhibition* out of internal organs: "the nervous systems of the characters have been externalized, as part of the reversal of the interior and exterior worlds. Highways, office blocks, faces, and street signs are perceived as if they were elements in a malfunctioning central nervous system."[23] Echoing Ballard, Sellars writes, "through the simple act of driving, we have become cyborgs by stealth, outsourcing mobility to the machine, which is controlled by the reactions of our brain and nervous system."[24] Having lost his wife to pneumonia in 1964, Ballard's began writing the despondently dark stories that would become *The Atrocity Exhibition*. The fully formed dystopia of *Crash* came not long after. Unlike the cyberpunks who followed him, Ballard's views of these near futures weren't as

---

22 Quoted in J.G. Ballard, *Extreme Metaphors: Collected Interviews,* eds. Simon Sellars and Dan O'Hara (London: Fourth Estate, 2012), 62.

23 Ballard, *The Atrocity Exhibition,* 76.

24 Simon Sellars, "Learning to Live with Aggressionless Cars," *Foreground,* April 15, 2021, https://www.foreground.com.au/transport/learning-to-live-with-aggressionless-cars/.

celebratory as they were cautionary: Dangerous Curves Ahead. Slow Down.[25]

Mistaken Algorithms

Ballard's warnings notwithstanding, still we persist. Cinema is our most viable and enduring form of design fiction. More than any other medium, it lets us peer into possible futures projected from the raw materials of the recent past, simulate scenes based on new visions via science and technology, gauge our reactions, and adjust our plans accordingly. These visions are equipment for living in a future heretofore unseen. As the video artist Bill Viola puts it,

> the implied goal of many of our efforts, including technological development, is the eradication of signal-to-noise ratio, which in the end is the ultimate transparent state where there is no perceived difference between the simulation and the reality, between ourselves and the other. We think of two lovers locked in a single ecstatic embrace. We think of futuristic descriptions of direct stimulation to the brain to evoke experiences and memories.[26]

When we think of the future, the images we conjure end up on the screen.

With only one adaptation, director David Cronenberg proved perhaps Ballard's most effective cinematic interpreter. Roger Ebert said of his version of *Crash,* "it's like a porno movie made by a computer: it downloads gigabytes of information about sex, it discovers our love affair with cars, and it combines them in a

---

25   See Simon Sellars, *Applied Ballardianism: Memoir from a Parallel Universe* (Falmouth: Urbanomic, 2018). Michel de Certeau once wrote, "books are only metaphors of the body." Ballard often seemed to be crash-testing that idea. Michel de Certeau, *The Practice of Everyday Life* (Berkeley: University of California Press, 1984), 140.

26   Bill Viola, *Reasons for Knocking at an Empty House: Writings 1973–1994* (Cambridge: The MIT Press, 1995).

mistaken algorithm.'²⁷ These visions of intimate machines give both versions of *Crash* a sense of malign prophecy. Before *Crash* in 1996, an adaptation Ballard loved, Cronenberg had already established himself as the preeminent body-horror director with such films as *The Brood* (1979), *Scanners* (1981), *Videodrome* (1983), *The Fly* (1986), *Dead Ringers* (1988), and *Naked Lunch* (1991). Jessica Kiang writes of *Crash*, "Koteas's Vaughan explains that his project is 'the reshaping of the human body through technology,' a pretty perfect summation of a recurring theme in the first half of Cronenberg's career, best exemplified by his 1983 masterpiece, *Videodrome*."²⁸

In *Videodrome,* CIVIC-TV's satellite dish operator, Harlan (played by Peter Dvorsky) pirates the signal of a plotless show of pure violence called "Videodrome" being beamed from bands in between. In search of unique programming for the station, Max Renn (played by James Woods) authorizes its rebroadcast. Renn soon finds that the footage is not faked and is PR for a socio-political movement weaponizing the signal for mind control. Professor Brian O'Blivion (played by Jack Creley) helped develop the signal to unify the minds of the viewers. *Videodrome* gave him a brain tumor and subsequent hallucinations. He sees the resultant state as a higher form of reality. As his daughter explains, "he saw it as part of the evolution of man as a technological animal. [...] He became convinced that public life on television was more real than private life in the flesh. He

---

27 Roger Ebert, "'Crash' (1997)," *RogerEbert.com,* March 21, 1997, http://www.
    rogerebert.com/reviews/crash-1997.

28 Jessica Kiang, "'Crash': The Wreck of the Century," *The Criterion Collec-
    tion,* December 1, 2020, https://www.criterion.com/current/posts/7206-
    crash-the-wreck-of-the-century. She continues, "so, when Vaughan later
    retracts that statement, calling it 'a crude sci-fi concept that floats on the
    surface and doesn't threaten anybody,' it's hard not to see Cronenberg slyly
    denigrating his own back catalog, or at least marking in boldface the end
    of his ongoing engagement with it. Sure enough, with the exception of a
    watered-down workout in 1999's *eXistenZ, Crash* does represent a move
    away from the gleefully visceral grotesqueries of his early career, toward
    the more refined psychological grotesqueries of his twenty-first-century
    output."

wasn't afraid to let his body die."[29] He tells Max, "the battle for the mind of North America will be fought in the video arena, the *Videodrome*. The television screen is the retina of the mind's eye. Therefore, the screen is part of the physical structure of the brain. Therefore, whatever appears on the television screen emerges as raw experience for those who watch it. Therefore, television is reality, and reality is less than television."[30] It doesn't take long for the reality in this film to devolve into a hallucinatory state itself. As the dialog of the last scene goes, "to become the new flesh you have to kill the old flesh. Don't be afraid. Don't be afraid to let your body die. […] Watch. I'll show you how. It's easy. Long live the new flesh. Long live the new flesh."[31]

Videodrome is another example of the view of the body — and the brain inside it — as an antenna, picking up signals from television broadcasts and the airwaves themselves. As Warren Ellis once said, "if you believe that your thoughts originate inside your brain, do you also believe that television shows are made inside your television set?"[32] It seems relevant here also that Albert Einstein wrote the preface to Upton Sinclair's aptly titled 1930 treatise on telepathy, *Mental Radio,* which he described as being "of high psychological interest."[33] These are visions of escape through media, escape routes as media.

The character of Professor Brian O'Blivion was inspired by Marshall McLuhan, one of Cronenberg's college professors at the University of Toronto.[34] McLuhan famously appeared in a

29 David Cronenberg, dir., *Videodrome* (Alliance Communications, 1983).
30 Ibid.
31 Ibid.
32 From Ellis's defunct newsletter, quoted in Steven Shaviro, "Swimming Pool," *The Pinocchio Theory,* January 29, 2004, http://www.shaviro.com/Blog/?m=200401.
33 See Upton Sinclair, *Mental Radio: Does It Work, and How?* (Springfield: Charles C. Thomas, 1930), ix. Arthur Koestler called this a "symbolic act." Arthur Koestler, *The Roots of Coincidence: An Excursion into Parapsychology* (New York: Vintage, 1972), 50.
34 Ben Sherlock, "Long Live the New Flesh: 10 Behind the Scenes Facts about 'Videodrome,'" *Screen Rant,* August 1, 2020, https://screenrant.com/videodrome-movie-behind-scenes-facts/.

fourth-wall-breaking scene in *Annie Hall* (1977), where Woody Allen introduces him, speaking directly to the camera. That wall is the contested barrier of *Videodrome*. McLuhan's concerns about information overload and media reconfiguring our brains were not lost on Cronenberg, and Cronenberg's own concerns about the technological manipulation of brains and bodies weren't lost on his son either.

An expectedly large leap from body horror's origins in Mary Shelley's 1818 novel, *Frankenstein,* Brandon Cronenberg's 2020 film, *Possessor,* nonetheless concerns itself with manipulating flesh for murderous ends. Tasya Vos (played by Andrea Riseborough) hijacks bodies via their brains in order to carry out assassinations unscathed. Through an advanced neurological interface, she takes over another's body. Once the hit is in, she returns to her own by forcing the host to kill themselves. Like the Sunken Place in Jordan Peele's *Get Out* (2017), the cognitive contrivance in Possessor pushes one consciousness out of the way of another. Once in control of a new body in a new social context, the operative is able to perform heinous acts in their name — namely murder-suicides.

When Tasya returns from a mission, she has to recalibrate to the real world in her own body. One of the tests for this debriefing process involves a number of analog, personal totems. This tests the idea that the analog world is our native environment as humans, as we all slide into ever more-digital worlds. The first of Tasya's totems in the test is her grandfather's pipe. The second is a mounted butterfly. "This is an old souvenir," she remembers. "I killed her one day when I was a child and… I felt guilty… I still feel guilty."[35] As much as the butterfly and her memory of it serve to anchor her here, her guilt is the real anchor. Guilt is our private connection to others.

Even so, when one of her victims, Colin Tate (played by Christopher Abbott), manages to wrest control of his body from her, he calls her agency into question. Using his fragmented ac-

---

35   Brandon Cronenberg, dir., *Possessor* (Rhombus Media, 2020).

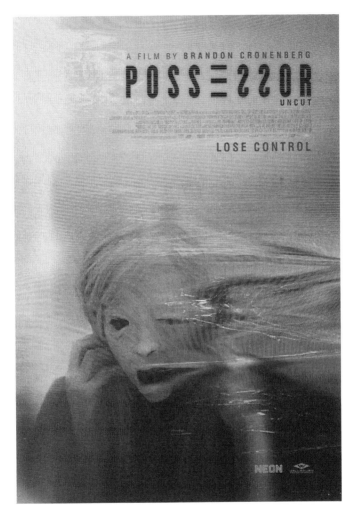

Fig. 6. Predator Things: Brandon Cronenberg's *Possessor,* 2020.

cess to Taysa's memories, Colin manages to find her home, infiltrates it, and berates her husband:

> just think, one day your wife is cleaning the cat litter and she gets a worm in her, and that worm ends up in her brain. The next thing that happens is she gets an idea in there, too. And it's hard to say whether that idea is really hers or it's just the worm. And it makes her do certain things. Predator things. Eventually, you realize that she isn't the same person anymore. She's not the person that she used to be. It's gotta make you wonder whether you're really married to her or married to the worm.[36]

Verifying the source of a message or an idea is a struggle even outside of our heads. When they pop in unannounced, there's no way to know where they came from. It makes it difficult to care about the sender.

At the end of the movie when Taysa encounters the dead butterfly again during recalibration, she says she no longer feels guilty for killing it.

Yale University professor Dr. José M.R. Delgado's 1969 book, *Physical Control of the Mind: Toward a Psychocivilized Society,* provides an intriguing precursor to Cronenberg's film. In this book, Delgado outlines the methodology for Cronenberg's fictional conceit. Delgado wrote, "by means of ESB (electrical stimulation of the brain) it is possible to control a variety of functions — a movement, a glandular secretion, or a specific mental manifestation, depending on the chosen target."[37] While admitting that the brain is protected by layers of bone and membrane, he illustrates how easily it is accessed through the senses, drawing convenient comparisons between garage-door openers and two-way radios, and light waves and optical nerves. Direct brain interfaces through implants have existed since the 1930s when

---

36 Ibid.
37 José M.R. Delgado, *Physical Control of the Mind: Toward a Psychocivilized Society* (New York: Harper & Row, 1969), 80.

Fig. 7. Wetware meets hardware: Godflesh's *Selfless,* 1994.

W.R. Hess wired a cat's hypothalamus with electrodes. Hess was able to induce everything from urination and defecation to hunger, thirst, and extreme excitement.

Given the limited viability of such technology during the writing of Delgado's book, he speculates the future of what he calls "stimoceivers," writing, "it is reasonable to speculate that in the near future the stimoceiver may provide the essential link from man to computer to man, with reciprocal feedback between neurons and instruments which represents a new orientation for the medical control of neurophysiological functions."[38] Though Delgado's stimoceivers are becoming more and more

---

38 Ibid., 91.

viable, they still require the mind and the machine to adapt to each other.

The cover of *Selfless,* Godflesh's 1994 record, is a picture of a human nerve cells growing on a microchip. It's a picture of what's called neuromorphic computing, a field of artificial intelligence that goes beyond using models of the human brain to physically harness its computing power, either by growing cells on chips or putting chips in brains. In August of 2020, Elon Musk debuted Tesla's Neuralink brain implant, demonstrating the device on three unsuspecting pigs.[39] The small, coinlike device reads neural activity, and Musk hopes they will eventually write it as well, connecting brains and computers in a completely new way, mirroring neurons and computer chips. The Neuralink team hopes the devices will correct injuries, bypass pain, record and restore memories, and enable telepathy. As Ballard and the Cronenbergs warned us, one person's mind-altering technology is another's absolute nightmare. "In Godflesh," Daniel Lukes writes, "the human is subsumed into the machine as an act of spiritual transubstantiation."[40] Computer processors open another path out of the body.

Answering Machines

"Welcome to the world of Pinecone Computers," Miles Harding (played by Lenny Von Dohlen) reads from a computer manual in *Electric Dreams* (1984). "This model will learn with you, so

---

39 See Leah Crane, "Elon Musk Demonstrated a Neuralink Brain Implant in a Live Pig," *NewScientist,* August 29, 2020, https://www.newscientist.com/article/2253274-elon-musk-demonstrated-a-neuralink-brain-implant-in-a-live-pig. See also Melissa Heikkilä, "Machines Can Read Your Brain. There's Little That Can Stop Them," *Politico,* August 31, 2021, https://www.politico.eu/article/machines-brain-neurotechnology-neuroscience-privacy-neurorights-protection.

40 Daniel Lukes, "Black Metal Machine: Theorizing Industrial Black Metal," in *Helvete: A Journal of Black Metal Theory* 1, eds. Amelia Ishmacl et al. (Brooklyn: punctum books, 2013), 79.

type your name and press Enter key to begin."[41] Since the big-screen tales of the 1980s PC-era, the idea of machines merging with humans has been a tenacious trope in popular culture. In *Tron* (1982) Kevin Flynn (played by Jeff Bridges) was sucked through a laser into the digital realm. Wired to the testosterone, the hormone-driven juvenile geniuses of *Weird Science* (1985) set to work making the woman of their dreams. *WarGames* (1983) famously pit suburban whiz-kids against a machine hell-bent on launching global thermonuclear war. In *Electric Dreams* (1984), which is admittedly as much montage as it is movie, Miles (von Dohlen, who would go on to play the agora-phobic recluse Harold Smith in *Twin Peaks,* who kept obsessive journals of the townsfolks' innermost thoughts and dreams) attempts to navigate a bizarre love triangle between him, his comely neighbor, and his new computer.

From the jealous machine to falling in love with the machine, the theme remains pervasive. As artificial-intelligence researcher Ray Kurzweil writes of Spike Jonze's 2013 movie *Her,* "Jonze introduces another idea that I have written about [...] namely, AIs creating an avatar of a deceased person based on their writings, other artifacts and people's memories of that person."[42] In the near future of *Her,* Theodore Twombly (played by Joaquin Phoenix) writes letters for a living, letters between fathers and daughters, long-distance lovers, husbands, wives, and others. In doing so, he is especially susceptible to the power of narrative himself since his job involves the constant creation of believable, vicarious stories. His ability to immerse himself in the stories of others makes it that much easier for him to get lost in the love of his operating system, Samantha (voiced by Scarlett Johansson), as she constructs narratives to create her personal-ity, and thereby, their relationship.

---

41 Steve Barron, dir., *Electric Dreams,* written by Rusty Lemorande (Virgin Films, 1984).

42 Ray Kurzweil, "A Review of 'Her' by Ray Kurzweil," *Kurzweil.com,* Febru-ary 10, 2014, https://www.kurzweilai.net/a-review-of-her-by-ray-kurzweil.

Cognitive scientist Douglas Hofstadter calls our imbuing machines with more intelligence than they have — even when we know better — "The ELIZA Effect," after Joseph Weizenbaum's text-based psychoanalytic computer program, ELIZA. Hofstadter writes, "the most superficial of syntactic tricks convinced some people who interacted with ELIZA that the program actually understood everything that they were saying, sympathized with them, even *empathized* with them."[43] ELIZA was written at MIT by Weizenbaum in the mid-1960s, but its effects linger on. "Like a tenacious virus that constantly mutates," Hofstadter continues, "the Eliza effect seems to crop up over and over again in AI in ever-fresh disguises, and in subtler and subtler forms."[44] In the first chapter of Sherry Turkle's *Alone Together,* she extends the idea to our amenability to new technologies, including artificial intelligence, embodied or otherwise: "and true to the ELIZA effect, this is not so much because the robots are ready but because we are."[45]

More germane to *Her* is a program called KARI, which stands for "Knowledge Acquiring and Response Intelligence." According to Dominic Pettman's first and only conversation with KARI, as described in his 2013 book, *Look at the Bunny,* there's a long way to go before any of us are falling in love with our computers.[46] After interacting with a similar bot online, Jonze agrees. "For the first, maybe, twenty seconds of it," he says, "I had this real buzz — I'd say 'Hey, hello,' and it would say 'Hey, how are you?,' and it was like whoa… this is trippy. After twenty seconds, it quickly fell apart and you realized how it actually works, and it wasn't that impressive. But it was still, for twenty seconds, really exciting. The more people that talked to it, the smarter it

43 Douglas Hofstadter, *Fluid Concepts and Creative Analogies: Computer Models of the Fundamental Mechanisms of Thought* (New York: Basic Books, 1995), 158.

44 Ibid.

45 Sherry Turkle, *Alone Together: Why We Expect More from Technology and Less from Each Other* (New York: Basic Books, 2011), 24–25.

46 See Dominic Pettman, *Look at the Bunny: Totem, Taboo, Technology* (Winchester: Zero Books, 2013).

Fig. 8. Theodore Twombly meets Samantha in Spike Jonze's *Her,* 2013. By kind permission of Spike Jonze.

got."[47] The author James Gleick comes to the conceit from the other side, writing, "I'd say *Her* is a movie about (the education of) an interesting woman who falls in love with a man who, though sweet, is mired in biology."[48] At one point in the movie, Samantha imagines the same fate for herself: "I could feel the weight of my body, and I was even fantasizing that I had an itch on my back — (she laughs) and I imagined that you scratched it for me — this is so embarrassing."[49] The dual feelings of being duped by technology and mired in biology sit on the cusp of the corporeal conundrum of what it means to be human, to have not only consciousness but also to have a body, as well as what having a body means.[50]

---

47 Quoted in Chris Michael, "Spike Jonze on Letting 'Her' Rip and 'Being John Malkovich,'" *The Guardian,* September 9, 2013, https://www.theguardian.com/film/filmblog/2013/sep/09/spike-jonze-her-scarlett-johansson.

48 James Gleick on *Twitter,* February 16, 2014.

49 Spike Jonze, dir., *Her* (Annapurna, 2013).

50 As Hayles notes, "when information loses its body, equating humans and computers is especially easy." N. Katherine Hayles, *How We Became Posthuman: Virtual Bodies in Cybernetics, Literature, and Informatics* (Chicago: University of Chicago Press, 1999), 2.

Mechanical Matrimony

Where some see the whole mess of bodies and machines as one, big system. Others picture the airwaves themselves as extensions. "Telepresence," as envisioned by Pat Gunkel, Marvin Minsky, and others, sets out to achieve a sense of being there, transferring an embodied experience across space via telephone lines, satellites, and sensory feedback loops.[51] It sounds quaint in world where working from home is normal for many and at least an option for others, but McLuhan was writing about it in the 1960s, and Minsky and his lot were working on it in the 1970s.

Still others imagine a much more deliberate merging of the biological and the mechanical, postulating an uploading of human consciousness into the machines themselves. Known in robotic and artificial intelligence circles as "The Moravec Transfer," its namesake, the roboticist Hans Moravec, describes a human brain being uploaded, neuron by neuron, until it exists unperturbed inside a machine.[52] But Moravec wasn't the first to imagine such a transition. The cyberpunk novelist and mathematician Rudy Rucker outlined the process in his 1982 novel, *Software*. "It took me nearly a year to really figure out the idea," he writes, "simple as it now seems. I was studying the philosophy of computation at the University of Heidelberg, reading and pondering the essays of Alan Turing and Kurt Gödel."[53] Turing was an early inventor of computing systems and AI, best known for the Turing test, whereby an AI is considered to be truly thinking like a human if it can fool a human into thinking so. Gödel was a logician and mathematician, best known for his incompleteness theorem. Both were heavily influential on

---

51 See Marvin Minsky, "Telepresence," OMNI *Magazine,* June 1980, 45–52.
52 See Hans Moravec, *Mind Children: The Future of Robot and Human Intelligence* (Cambridge: Harvard University Press, 1988). For another early example, see G. Harry Stine, "The Bionic Brain," OMNI *Magazine,* July 1979, 84–86, 121–22.
53 Rudy Rucker, "Outer Banks & New York #1," *Rudy's Blog,* August 2, 2015, http://www.rudyrucker.com/blog/2015/08/02/outer-banks-new-york-1/.

the core concepts of computing and artificial intelligence. "It's some serious shit," Rucker writes of the process. "But I chose to present it in cyberpunk format. So, no po-faced serious, analytic-type, high literary mandarins are ever gonna take my work seriously."[54] In Rucker's story, a robot saves its creator by uploading his consciousness into a robot.

NASA's own Robert Jastrow wrote in 1984 that uploading our minds into machines is the be-all of evolution and would make us immortal. He wrote,

> at last the human brain, ensconced in a computer, has been liberated from the weakness of the mortal flesh. [...] The machine is its body; it is the machine's mind. [...] It seems to me that this must be the mature form of intelligent life in the Universe. Housed in indestructible lattices of silicon, and no longer constrained in the span of its years by the life and death cycle of a biological organism, such a kind of life could live forever.[55]

In the 2014 movie *Transcendence* (2014), Dr. Will Caster (played by Johnny Depp) and his wife Evelyn (played by Rebecca Hall) do just that. Caster is terminally ill and on the verge of offloading his mortal shell. Once his mind is uploaded into a quantum computer connected to the internet, Caster becomes something less than himself and something more simultaneously. It's the chronic consciousness question: What is it about you that makes you *you*? Is it still there once all of your bits are transferred into a new vessel? The Casters' love was strong enough for them to try and find out.

---

54 Ibid.
55 Robert Jastrow, *The Enchanted Loom: Mind in the Universe* (New York: Simon & Schuster, 1984), 166–67.

Brick Body Kids Still Daydream[56]

In the desert along the border between California and Nevada, corporations are building server farms, giant structures meant to house machines instead of humans. These buildings don't look much different from any other nondescript industrial space from the outside, but they don't like traditional buildings on the inside. They are unwelcoming, with little to offer humans. "For the employees there are only small rooms to relax in," says the architect Rem Koolhaas. "They are paneled with Norwegian wood and Buddha statues — a debased kind of humanism, if you will: A little bit of mysticism, a little bit of warmth. But not too much of anything"; in the face of these buildings without bodies, Koolhaas also adopts a systems view, that "the need for human comfort can be very limiting when it comes to the design of buildings."[57] These descriptions evoke the inhuman, industrial enclaves of Broadrick's native Birmingham, as well as the lyrics the Godflesh song, "Curse Us All": "You're an empty shell / Built from brick / A living hell / Spewing shit."[58]

If Kubrick and Spielberg's 2001 movie *AI: Artificial Intelligence* can be read as an allegory for gay children being accepted by their parents,[59] what sociological anxieties can we superimpose over *Her* and *Transcendence*? I am admittedly a lapsed student of AI, having dropped out of the University of Georgia's Artificial Intelligence masters program midway through my first semester there in 1999. My interest in AI lies in the weird ways that consciousness and creation butt heads in the midst of such advanced technologies. As Jonze himself puts it, "a lot of

---

56 Open Mike Eagle, *Brick Body Kids Still Daydream* [LP] (Tucson: Mello Music Group, 2017).

57 Quoted in Johannes Boehme, "An Interview with Rem Koolhaas," *The Believer,* January 31, 2020, https://culture.org/an-interview-with-rem-koolhaas/.

58 Godflesh, *A World Lit Only by Fire* [LP] (London: Avalanche Recordings, 2014).

59 See Chris Kraus, *Video Green: Los Angeles Art and the Triumph of Nothingness* (New York: Semiotext(e), 2004), 182.

the feelings you have about relationships or about technology are often contradictory."[60]

If bodies didn't exist, we would have to invent them. Hans Moravec writes,

> a human would likely fare poorly in such a cyberspace. Unlike the streamlined artificial intelligences that zip about, making discoveries and deals, rapidly reconfiguring themselves to efficiently handle changing data, a human mind would lumber about in a massively inappropriate body simulation, like a deep-sea diver plodding through a troupe of acrobatic dolphins. Every interaction with the world would first be analogized into a recognizable quasiphysical form: other programs might be presented as animals, plants, or demons, data items as books or treasure chests, accounting entries as coins or gold. Maintaining the fictions will increase the cost of doing business and decrease responsiveness, as will operating the mind machinery that reduces the physical simulations into mental abstractions in the human mind.[61]

We are the ghosts in these machines.[62] Our merging nuptials, to have, to hold, and to haunt. Simon Sellars continues, "the question no longer concerns a primitive posthumanism but a new singularity, for here is the moment in which the machine completely surpasses the human and absorbs it until there is nothing left."[63] Given a choice between the physical and the digital,

---

60 Quoted in Michael, "Spike Jonze on Letting 'Her' Rip and 'Being John Malkovich.'"

61 Hans Moravec, "The Senses Have No Future," in *The Virtual Dimension: Architecture, Representation, and Crash Culture,* ed. John Beckmann (New York: Princeton Architectural Press, 1998), 94.

62 Mark Fisher wrote, "there are ghosts in the machine, and we are they, and they are we." Mark Fisher, *The Weird and the Eerie* (London: Repeater Books, 2016), 109.

63 Sellars, "Learning to Live with Aggressionless Cars."

many of us would go ones-and-zeros in a final heartbeat. Per-haps we will anyway.[64]

"Machines are now unavoidable," Ollivier Dyens writes, "not only when we look for understanding of the world's scientific phenomena but also when we search for signs of God in distant nebula. We are cyborgs, for only with machines can we face the sun."[65] Our desires to escape not just the confines of our bodies but the bricks of the council block are at odds with their very limits. Kiang adds, "so here we are in the future that *Crash* re-fused to envisage, in which technophilia of a different, digital flavor has come to make the film's preoccupation with bodies melding with machines seem analog and almost quaint."[66] We are still more likely to be swallowed up by cars than computers. No matter the manner, if the mind can be unembodied from its body and reembodied in another vessel — machine or other-wise — where else might it venture?

---

64 As Terence McKenna put it to Erik Davis, "the best answer I've gotten yet is out of Don DeLillo's *Underworld,* where the nun discovers that when you die you become your Web site." Quoted in Erik Davis, "Terrence Mc-Kenna's Last Trip," WIRED, May 1, 2000, https://www.wired.com/2000/05/mckenna/.

65 Ollivier Dyens, *Metal and Flesh: The Evolution of Man: Technology Takes Over,* trans. Evan J. Bibbee and Ollivier Dyens (Cambridges: MIT Press, 2001), 14. See also Gerald Raunig, *Dividuum: Machinic Capitalism and Molecular Revolution* (New York: Semiotext(e), 2016), passim, esp. 109–14.

66 Kiang, "'Crash.'" She continues, "or at least it would, if *Crash* did not also repel any attempt to sentimentalize or nostalgize it. Ballard again: 'Human beings have a terrible temptation to imagine a happier past.' But Cronen-berg's *Crash* will not allow us to engage in any such delusional project. Even now that its ticking engine has cooled, its upturned wheels have ceased spinning, and its mangled frame is partly grown over by the grass of the intervening decades, it remains exactly as fascinating, salutary, and instructive as a spectacular wreck on the side of the highway, and just about as lovable. But then, what *Crash*'s most passionate advocates feel for the movie has never been love — soft, warm, fleeting — but fetish, a cold, deathless, chromium fetish that will last forever. Welcome to the cult."

4

Rapture
Through Grace and Time

"Prophecy is dirty and ragged."
— Vaughan in David Cronenberg, *Crash*[1]

"The Rapture and the Singularity share one thing in common: they can never be verified by the living."
— Jaron Lanier, *You Are Not a Gadget*[2]

"In the church of my heart, the choir's in flames."
— Vladimir Mayakovsky, "A Cloud in Trousers"[3]

As if tuned to the mourning tones of some celestial monochord, Tom G. Warrior's guitar thunders like planets wobbling off their axes, ripped from their orbits. Warrior has helmed pioneering proto-black metal bands Hellhammer and Celtic Frost, as well as the more recent and more experimental Triptykon. On Celtic Frost's "A Dying God Coming into Human Flesh," the first single

---

1   David Cronenberg, dir., *Crash* (Los Angeles: Universal Pictures, 1996).
2   Jaron Lanier, *You Are Not a Gadget: A Manifesto* (New York: Alfred A. Knopf, 2010), 26.
3   Vladimir Mayakovsky, "A Cloud in Trousers," in *Russian Poetry: The Modern Period,* eds. John Glad and Daniel Weissbort (Iowa City: University of Iowa Press, 1978), 14.

73

Fig. 9. Only Death is Real: Celtic Frost. Photo by Sergio Archetti. Promotional photo.

from their 2006 comeback record, *Monotheist,* bassist Martin Ain sings, "frozen is heaven and frozen is hell, and I am dying in this living human shell" before Warrior comes in to wail the refrain, "I am a dying god coming into human flesh,"[4] over and over into the outer rings.

The Rapture, the leaving of earth through heavenly salvation, is played out here in reverse, a divine degradation. Instead of a dying god caged in human flesh, in Rapture, the corporeal body is left behind for the eternity beyond. "I heard someone once say that 'music is the voice of God'," Godflesh's Justin Broadrick says. "In that sense, it's something that can get inside of you and move you spiritually on a communication level. The word 'God' conjures something immense and inconceivable. The 'flesh' part

---

4   Martin Eric Ain, "A Dying God Coming into Human Flesh," on *Monotheist* [LP], recorded by Celtic Frost (Dortmund: Century Media Records, 2006). The sentiment here recalls Thomas Ligotti's contention that God created humans as a form of suicide. See Thomas Ligotti, *The Conspiracy against the Human Race* (New York: Hippocampus Press, 2010), 19.

is what affects you on a physical level."[5] Extreme sounds at ex-treme volumes, like those performed by bands like Celtic Frost and Godflesh, bypass the brain and affect the body directly. In a statement Warrior and Ain would certainly agree with, Broad-rick adds, "our music is loud and destructive."[6]

In theorizing such a spiritual sound, a "celestial monochord," seventeenth century English occult philosopher Robert Fludd's aim was not only to sonically order the cosmos but also to es-tablish a god-sound preceding all others. Adam McLean terms Fludd's idea "hermetic," writing: "the hermetic world view held by such as Robert Fludd, pictured a great chain of being link-ing our inner spark of consciousness with all the facets of the Great World. There was a grand platonic metaphysical clock-work, as it were, through which our inner world was linked by means of a hierarchy of beings and planes to the highest unity of the Divine."[7] The eleventh treatise of the *Corpus Hermeticum* declares that "unless you make yourself equal to god, you can-not understand god."[8] In his own book *Techgnosis,* Erik Davis describes the *Hermetica* as "an esoteric patchwork of alchemi-cal, astrological, and mystical writings compiled from the sec-ond to the fourth centuries C.E., the *Hermetica* was mythi-cally considered to be a single work composed by [...] Hermes Trismegistus."[9] In 1617 Fludd wrote,

from the symphonious influence on the heavens, then it aris-es that the magnet attracts iron, amber silver, the sea-crab

---

5   Quoted in "FAQ," *Godflesh.com,* https://godflesh.com/faq.html.

6   Ibid. Broadrick has cited "Anything Is Mine" from Godflesh's *Selfless* as a "blatant Celtic Frost" rip-off. See Albert Mudrian, "Godflesh's Justin Broadrick: 'I Never Feel Comfortable at Any Festival,'" *Decibel Magazine,* October 17, 2018, https://www.decibelmagazine.com/2018/10/17/godfleshs-justin-broadrick-i-never-feel-comfortable-at-any-festival.

7   Adam McLean, "Quantum Consciousness," *Alchemy Web Site,* https://www.alchemywebsite.com/quantum.html.

8   Brian R. Copenhaver, trans., *Corpus Hermeticum* (Cambridge: Cambridge University Press, 1992), 41.

9   Erik Davis, *Techgnosis: Myth, Magic, and Mysticism in the Age of Informa-tion* (New York: Harmony, 1998), 27.

(*carabe*), hairs and straw, and the magnetic salve the nature of a wounded man, each holding the other in extraordinary affection. Their dissonant influence also produces the antipathy and discord of things, such as between lamb and wolf, dormouse and cat, the cock's crow and the lion, the sight of basilisk or *catablepas* and man, and many others. Now the concords of divine music draw similar things to them for their protection, and the discords of the same drive away and put to flight dissimilar and contrary things for the same purpose.[10]

And what are the lumbering dead but the leftover meat of transcendence, the cast-off husks of rapture? The spirit resides more in the head than the heart.[11] The zombie is the result of the mind permanently leaving the body on a lower plane. Space-time doesn't ground, it suspends.[12] In Fludd's view, these bodies are no longer led by the life-giving music of the cosmos, radio antennae sucked up by the signal, receivers received at last.

Blank Solitude

Again, what about the inverse, the body tuned to a different tune? In Jonathan Glazer's stunning 2014 film, *Under the Skin,* Scarlett Johansson plays a man-eating, alien visitor slipped into a human sleeve, a body snatcher of a different kind. Lucy Bolton describes the film as "a viewing experience that is mediated by the emotional, moral and corporeal alien eye."[13] While Glazer's

---

10 Robert Fludd, "On the Occult and Wondrous Effects of Secret Music," in *Tractatus Apologeticus Integritatum Societatis de Rosea Crucis defendens* (Leiden, 1617). See also Eugene Thacker, "Sound of the Abyss," in *Melancology: Black Metal Theory and Ecology,* ed. Scott Wilson (Winchester: Zero Books, 2014), 182.

11 Smith, *The Body,* 297.

12 See Kirk J. Schneider, *Horror and the Holy: Wisdom-Teachings of the Monster Tale* (Chicago: Open Court, 1993), esp. 9–11.

13 Lucy Bolton, "'Under the Skin' and the Affective Alien Body," paper presented at *Film-Philosophy Conference 2014: A World of Cinemas,* University of Glasgow, Glasgow, UK, January 2, 2014, 1.

adaptation is an intriguing interpretation, Jonathan Faber's original novel is versatile, lending itself to many others. Taken in tandem though, they inform each other. "[The book] was a jumping-off point," Glazer tells Chris Alexander at *Fangoria*.[14] "*Under the Skin* is trying to represent something kind of unimaginable — this infinite and alien entity," he says. "It's not something for words, really. It shouldn't be explained away. Our intention was to protect its alienness."[15] That alienness is key. Mark Fisher wrote about the scene in the movie where Johansson's alien sees itself in the mirror: "it is clear now that the mirror scene redoubles the 'ordinary' self-objectification that happens when we look in the mirror: the alien is not looking at herself, but at the human body she is wearing."[16]

Somehow so far in the twenty-first century, Johansson has emerged in film as the ultimate person, the final girl of all the horror that is human. As mentioned last chapter, she voiced Samantha, the operating-system love interest of Theodore Twombly, in Spike Jonze's *Her*. She shook Bob Harris (played by Bill Murray) out of a late-life lull in Sophia Coppola's *Lost in Translation* (2003). She repeated Logan's Run in *The Island* (2005). She transcends her own brain and body in *Lucy* (2014). She starred in the live-action version of *Ghost in the Shell* (2017). And she was Natasha Romanoff, the perfect cyborg assassin in *Black Widow* (2021). In short, when we think of machine-aided human perfection, Johansson is what we picture. Perhaps the flaws between us and an embodied computing machine are mirrored in the unachievable image of the American blonde.

In *Cool Memories IV,* Jean Baudrillard wrote, "the photographic lens makes you immediately indifferent to yourself — you inwardly play dead. In the same way, the presence of television cameras makes what you are saying seem alien or

---

14 Quoted in Chris Alexander, "The Skin He's In," *Fangoria Magazine* 322, May 2014, 43.

15 Ibid., 45.

16 Mark Fisher, *The Weird and the Eerie* (London: Repeater Books, 2016), 108.

a matter of indifference."[17] Johansson begins an interview with Tim Noakes at *Dazed & Confused* magazine reading from Baudrillard's *America,* his collection about feeling like an alien in a foreign land. "Smile and others will smile back," she reads. "Smile to show how transparent, how candid you are. Smile if you have nothing to say. Most of all, do not hide the fact you have nothing to say nor your total indifference to others. Let this emptiness, this profound indifference shine out spontaneously in your smile."[18] Further down that same page, Baudrillard wrote, "the skateboarder with his Walkman, the intellectual working on his word-processor, the Bronx breakdancer whirling frantically in the Roxy, the jogger and the bodybuilder: everywhere, whether in regard to the body or the mental faculties, you find the same blank solitude, the same narcissistic refraction."[19]

Johansson feels that alienness herself. "When I finish work," she says, "I just want to get as far away from it as possible. It's like, 'Okay, we're done, let me try to regain my sense of self!'[…] I've certainly had roles which have become all-encompassing, when I've been like, 'Whoa, where's my life?,' and felt like the floor had been swept from underneath me. But the more experience you have, the less carried away you get."[20] As one review of *Under the Skin* parenthetically notes, "the film is nothing if not a knowing, subversive use of Johansson's celebrity and screen persona."[21] Celebrity itself produces cyborgs and aliens, prepped by trainers and stylists to become something more than human. They exist in an asymmetrical world, inflated to their audience by a system of interconnected media technologies on one side and alienated from them on the other.

---

17 Jean Baudrillard, *Cool Memories IV: 1995–2000,* trans. Chris Turner (New York: Verso, 2003), 107.

18 Jean Baudrillard, *America,* trans. Chris Turner (New York: Verso, 1988), 34.

19 Ibid.

20 Quoted in Tim Noakes, "Under the Skin of Scarlett Johansson," *Dazed & Confused,* March 12, 20124, https://www.dazeddigital.com/artsandculture/article/19057/1/under-the-skin-of-scarlett-johansson.

21 Realcaptainparsnips, "Their Bodies, Ourselves: Bodysnatching and the Male Gaze in Under the Skin," *Groupthink,* March 29, 2014.

Glazer says of her performance, "when she saw the film, she said to me that she didn't recognize what she was doing in it. […] [S]he said she had no idea what was going on in her mind at any point."[22] In a film so focused on alienation, it's interesting that Johansson felt it as the actor, as the alien, and as the viewer of this film. Through the lens, the narcissistic refraction: the alien gaze turned in upon itself.

High-Rise[23]

Belief in aliens is often used as a trope in television shows and movies to signify instability or insanity. The hundreds of accounts available consist largely of unverifiable evidence and arguments that are shaky at best. Many of the reporters of alien phenomena seek to find them. Their seeking is "wishful thinking" in the words of Carl Jung.[24] Yet, in his one book on the subject, *Flying Saucers,* Jung admits that "a purely psychological explanation is illusory, for a large number of observations point to natural phenomenon, or even a physical one."[25] He adds, "something is seen, but we don't know what."[26] The witnesses fall into a few distinct categories: those prone to fantasy and self-delusion (of course), those who are awake and outdoors at odd hours (security staff and police officers), and those attuned to the skies (pilots and air traffic controllers).

The descriptions in the many reports I've read seem either embellished or evasive, imbued with insistence depending on how much the witness wants to believe. There's just no way to tell if anyone has actually seen anything. The very designation "unidentified flying object" is so ambiguous as to be nearly useless. The Condon Report from 1969, the culmination of all of the Air Force's investigations into so-called sightings — Project Sign,

---

22 Quoted in Alexander, "The Skin He's In," 130.
23 J.G. Ballard, *High-Rise: A Novel* (London: Jonathan Cape, 1975).
24 Carl G. Jung, *Man and His Symbols* (New York: Bantam, 1964), 69.
25 Carl G. Jung, *Flying Saucers: A Modern Myth of Things Seen in the Skies* (Princeton: Princeton University Press, 1978), 132.
26 Ibid., 136.

Project Grudge, Project Blue Book — defines a UFO as follows: "an unidentified flying object is here defined as the stimulus for a report made by one or more individuals of something seen in the sky (or an object thought to be capable of flight but seen when landed on earth) which the observer could not identify as having ordinary natural origin, and which seemed to him [sic] sufficiently puzzling that he [sic] undertook to make a report of it."[27] In filing the report, one is saying that the sighting was "sufficiently puzzling" enough to file the report. It's not so much defining what a UFO is as it's defining what filing the report means. The Air Force either took the reports seriously enough or just received so many of them that they had to make them the subject of several official projects. Ex-Project Blue Book member Fritz Werner (not his real name) said in an interview that Blue Book existed because the Air Force "was getting too much publicity and there were too many people, other than official people seeing things and reporting them."[28]

Upon allegedly returning from other planets, many early alien contactees believe they've been bestowed a mission to save this one. The earliest cases, the messages had to do with advancing technology to aid in our survival. Given the onset of the Cold War, contactees from the 1950s were increasingly "concerned with the effects of atomic power, war, pollution, and the need for the human family to come together."[29] Some were even touted as new messiahs, sent to save us all from our own, self-styled destruction.

In the case of cults like Heaven's Gate, UFO enthusiasts build religions around their search for truth. Balch and Taylor's germinal 1976 *Psychology Today* article "Salvation in a UFO" describes

---

27 Edward Condon, *Final Report of the Scientific Study of Unidentified Flying Objects* (New York: Dutton, 1969), 9.

28 Quoted in Kevin D. Randle, *A History of UFO Crashes* (New York: Avon Books, 1995), 58.

29 J. Gordon Melton, "The Contactees: A Survey," in *The Gods Have Landed: New Religions from Other Worlds,* ed. James R. Lewis (Albany: University of New York Press, 1995), 8. See also Curtis G. Fuller, *Proceedings of the First International UFO Congress* (New York: Warner Books, 1980).

Heaven's Gate members as "metaphysical seekers": "before join-
ing [Heaven's Gate], members of the UFO cult had organized
their lives around the quest for truth. Most defined themselves
as spiritual seekers."[30] In and out of other such groups before set-
tling with Heaven's Gate, the founders and members could all be
described as seekers. In his book, *Heaven's Gate: America's UFO
Religion,* Benjamin E. Zeller studies the subject through religious scholarship. Contra the media's reports of Heaven's Gate's
mass suicides in March of 1997, Zeller writes that they "envisioned the Earth not as merely something to graduate from, but
something to hate, human bodies not merely things top evolve
out of, but vehicles to willfully destroy through suicide."[31] They
saw this destruction not as suicide, but as "graduation from an
unwanted terrestrial existence on an unbearable planet in disa-
greeable bodies."[32] The belief that in synchronized suicide, they
were to board a UFO following the Hale-Bopp comet to salvation
came from the New Age arm of their religion. "Heaven's Gate
emerged out of two theological worlds: Evangelical Christianity and the New Age movement, particularly the element of the
New Age movement concerned with alien visitation and extraterrestrial contact."[33] Loosely speaking, UFO religions culminate
in a cafeteria-style belief system: all-you-can-eat at one end and
monastic abstinence at the other. No matter their diet, saviors
imbued with special knowledge or unwitting cyborgs implanted
with alien technology, abductees rarely entertain the option of
being wrong.

Where Jung saw the UFO phenomenon as seekers longing
for a more complete life, Michael Heim sees it as "technology

---

30 Robert W. Balch and David Taylor, "Salvation in a UFO," *Psychology Today*
10, no. 5 (October 1976): 60.
31 Benjamin E. Zeller, *Heaven's Gate: America's UFO Religion* (New York: NYU
Press, 2014), 177.
32 Ibid., 178.
33 Ibid., 65. See also Mark Dery, *The Pyrotechnic Insanitarium: American Culture on the Brink* (New York: Grove Press, 1999), 247–57, and D.W. Pasulka,
American Cosmic: UFOs, Religion, Technology (Oxford: Oxford University
Press, 2019).

sickness."[34] Heim posited Alternate World Syndrome (AWS) as the switching between virtual and real worlds highlights the merging of technology with the human species, an extremely alien feeling we have yet to assimilate. It's the ontological jet lag that comes from visiting or envisioning another, alien world.[35] Violent video games are often scapegoated as desensitizing players to violence in the real world, and Franco "Bifo" Berardi supports Heim's AWS theory, writing, "it is not the content of the game, but the stimulation itself, that produces the effect of desensitization to the bodily experience of suffering and of pleasure."[36] Heim continues, echoing our concerns from last chapter: "the fascination and pain of the UFO phenomenon shows us only the first glimpse of our ultimate merger with technology."[37]

Sometimes when entities play, it's difficult to tell whether they're flirting or fighting.

Fickle Senses

The human brain's relationship with reality is not as steadfast as we'd like to think. The slightest ripple in our expectations can send us off one of many available edges. In his book, *The Conspiracy against the Human Race,* Thomas Ligotti paraphrases Peter Wessel Zapffe, writing, "consciousness is connected to the human brain in a way that makes the world appear to us as it appears and makes us appear to ourselves as we appear — that is, as 'selves' or as 'persons' strung together by memories, sensations, emotions, and so on."[38] Our consciousness is a cumulative collection of recollections, connections, habits, and hearsay.

---

34 Michael Heim, *Virtual Realism* (New York: Oxford University Press, 1998), 182.

35 See Michael Heim, *The Metaphysics of Virtual Reality* (Oxford: Oxford University Press, 1993).

36 Franco "Bifo" Berardi, *Heroes: Mass Murder and Suicide* (New York: Verso, 2015), 47.

37 Heim, *Virtual Realism,* 197.

38 Ligotti, *The Conspiracy against the Human Race,* 25.

When the continuity of those connections is corrupted, we are set adrift.

In Robert Guffey's book *Chameleo* (2015), his friend Dion has the continuity of his consciousness severely corrupted. Dion's reality is already shaky at best, so Guffey sets out to document and investigate the odd goings on around Dion. Quoting Theodore Sturgeon, Guffey says, "always ask the next question."[39] *Chameleo* turns on this very fulcrum: it is a series of next questions asked not necessarily until the questions are answered, but until all of the possibilities are exhausted.

Dion is followed, harassed, and interrogated by groups of people seen and unseen. Invisible little agents begin infiltrating his home after he is taken in for questioning about a load of missing night-vision goggles he had nothing to do with. These diminutive, invisible people sometimes appear as aberrations in Dion's peripheral vision. Imagine the painting of railroad tracks on the tops of trains. If you're looking at the train from above, you only see the tracks — unless you're watching very closely. Project Chameleo is based on a much more technologically advanced version of this very concept: invisibility by adaptive camouflage, like a texture-mapped, technicolor chameleon, obscuring a moving body. That's one of the simplest examples of the alien technology in this complex and confounding tale.

Like Robert Fludd's monochord, perhaps Heaven's Gate, Guffey's friend Dion, and our other seekers are just tuned in to an alien frequency unavailable to the rest of us, a channel from beyond. As Dr. Lilly wrote in 1972,

> presumably, there are many, many states of tuning for transmission and for reception. There are many, many bands of energy to which one can tune. There are bands emitted primarily by humans and received by humans. There are bands transmitted sand received by nonhuman intelligences on this

---

39 Robert Guffey, *Chameleo: A Strange but True Story of Invisible Spies, Heroin Addiction, and Homeland Security* (New York: O/R Books, 2015), 29.

planet, which we may or may not be able to tune in on. There are bands transmitted and received by entities who are vastly larger than us and who reside in other parts of the galaxy. Some reception can be from planetary transmissions; some can be from stars, suns, dust clouds, and so forth; some can be from humanlike intelligence somewhere in the galaxy and some can be from apparatus constructed by civilizations a thousand to a million years more advanced in their science.[40]

As below, so above.[41]

---

40 John C. Lilly, *The Center of the Cyclone: An Autobiography of Inner Space* (New York: The Julian Press, 1972), 142–43.

41 See Nicola Masciandaro, "On the Mystical Love of Black Metal," in *Floating Tomb: Black Metal Theory,* eds. Nicola Masciandaro and Edia Connole (Milan: Mimesis, 2015), 103, and Edia Connole, "Seven Propositions on the Secret Kissing of 333 Black Metal: OSKVLVM," in *Mors Mystica: Black Metal Theory Symposium,* eds. Edia Connole and Nicola Masciandaro (London: Schism, 2015), 347.

5

Drugs

Encounter Culture

"There are many, many more shades and colors to darkness than just black."
—Martin Eric Ain, Celtic Frost/Hellhammer[1]

"The important thing is to keep that smile on your face... even if you're drowning."
—Marly Temple, in John Sayles, *Sunshine State*[2]

"I'm dying."
"Is it blissful?"
"It's like a dream."
"I want to dream.
With you."
—Deafheaven, "Dream House"[3]

On top of the compound meanings of the word "Streetcleaner," "Godflesh" contains many connotations as well. "'Godflesh' is

---

1   Quoted in Sam Dunn and Scott McFadyen, *Metal Evolution,* episode 12, "Extreme Metal: The Lost Episode" (Banger Films, 2011).

2   John Sayles, dir., *Sunshine State* (Sony Pictures, 2002).

3   Deafheaven, *Sunbather* [LP] (Beverly: Deathwish, Inc., 2013).

the American Indian term for peyote," Justin Broadrick says, "but that really is kind of a coincidence. It's a coincidence that suits me just fine though."[4] Drugs and debauchery were an early part of Broadrick's life. He elaborates,

> early Godflesh was absolutely a product of my own environment, but it wasn't entirely the landscape outside the window, the concrete and the council estate; it was also to do with my childhood background, the way my mother was when I was young and what I was exposed to. I was exposed to drug-taking at an early age and a lot of intense partying. […] When we formed Godflesh, I was only 18 or something and still learning to deal with a lot of frustration, anger, love, hate…[5]

Broadrick's emotions parallel Dr. John C. Lilly's when returning to his body from an early acid trip. "I cried when I came back and found myself trapped in a body," Dr. Lilly lamented. "I didn't even know whose body it was at first. It was the sadness of reentry. I felt squashed."[6] As a neuroscientist and psychoanalyst, Dr. Lilly was interested in exiting the body through the mind. "In the province of the mind there are not limits," Dr. Lilly once wrote. "However, in the province of the body there are limits not to be transcended."[7] Lilly set out to mute his corporeal existence, to defy his earthbound master, to blaspheme his god, his flesh.

The image on the cover of *Streetcleaner* is a screenshot from Ken Russell's 1980 movie *Altered States.* The image, silhouettes

---

4   Quoted in "FAQ," *Godflesh.com,* https://godflesh.com/faq.html.
5   Quoted in Dimitri Nasrallah, "Justin Broadrick: Napalm Death – Godflesh – Techno Animal – Jesu – Pale Sketcher," *Exclaim!,* September 2010, http://exclaim.ca/Features/Timeline/JUSTIN_BROADRICK-Napalm_Death-Godflesh-Techno_Animal-Jesu-Pale_Sketcher.
6   Quoted in Judith Hooper, "Interview: John Lilly," *OMNI Magazine,* January 1983, 78.
7   John C. Lilly, *Programming and Metaprogramming in the Human Biocomputer: Theory and Experiments* (New York: The Julian Press, 1974).

Fig. 10. Altered States: Godflesh's *Streetcleaner*. Courtesy of Earache Records.

of a forest of crucifixions set against a sky of fire, is from one of the hallucination sequences in the film.[8] Adapted by Paddy Chayefsky from his novel, the movie follows a scientist attempting to escape his body through his mind, using sensory-deprivation tanks and mind-expanding substances. It's loosely based on Dr. Lilly's life and research. Exploring the extremes of neurophysiology, biophysics, and electronics, Lilly experimented on himself with isolation tanks, LSD, and later, ketamine. The movie

---

8   In the liner notes to the 2010 reissue of the record, Jonathan Selzer suggests that the image represents the dual themes of *Streetcleaner*, "endurance and purifying deliverance."

provided hours of acid-induced entertainment for the teenaged Broadrick. "Those sorts of trips we had, watching *Altered States* and *The Devils,* were such an influence on *Streetcleaner*," he remembers.[9]

While Chayefsky also wrote the screenplay, he was so unhappy with Russell's film he removed his name from the project.[10] Regardless of their creators' differences or incompatible tones, Chayefsky's novel and Russell's movie both depict the destination of their inner journeys as a nightmare, as climbing into the box with Pandora's evils and curses. Dr. Lilly saw tanking as a salve for our mortal sleeves, as no less than the sublimation of the self.[11]

One in the Chamber

Sensory-deprivation tanks are lightless boxes. The shallow water inside is saturated with enough salts to keep a body buoyant. The air and water are kept at a humid, human temperature. Nothing to see. Nothing to hear. Nothing to feel. Total isolation from sense data. Total isolation from everything else except your self.

"The tank is an awareness tool," said Dr. John Lilly in 1980, "like meditation, like Gestalt, like psychosynthesis, like psychotherapy, like a hammer or a saw, and I find tank work, like any

9 Quoted in Nasrallah, "Justin Broadrick."
10 Janet Maslin writes in *The New York Times,* "it's easy to guess why he and Mr. Russell didn't see eye to eye. The direction, without being mocking or campy, treats outlandish material so matter-of-factly that it often has a facetious ring. The screenplay, on the other hand, cries out to be taken seriously, as it addresses, with no particular sagacity, the death of God and the origins of man." Janet Maslin, "Screen: Ken Russell's 'Altered States'," *The New York Times,* December 25, 1980, https://www.nytimes.com/1980/12/25/arts/screen-ken-russells-altered-states.html.
11 This "sublimation" is what Freud referred to as "alloplastic" (external) compensation or manipulation. See Norman O. Brown, *Life against Death: The Psychoanalytical Meaning of History* (Middletown: Wesleyan University Press, 1959), 170; Mary Douglas, *Purity and Danger: An Analysis of the Concepts of Pollution and Taboo* (London: Routledge & Keegan Paul, 1966), 116–18.

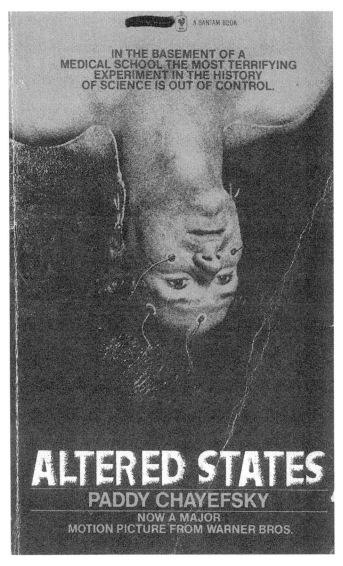

Fig. 11. Out of body, out of mind: Paddy Chayefsky's *Altered States,*
1978.

of the above tools, to be effective to the extent that I familiarize myself and practice with it. The tank assists a very simple function: [i]t allows us to expand our awareness of our internal state of being, of our internal flow."[12] Without physical stimuli, the brain begins to improvise. Without practice, its improvisations can run astray.[13]

Paddy Chayefsky described his own isolation-tank experience as "a warm return to your mother's womb."[14] In *OMNI Magazine* in 1980, writer John Gorman describes his inner visit differently:

> the darkness around me remains the same whether my eyes are open or closed. Still, it seems easier to close my eyes. At first, I feel time passing. My thoughts are logical and body-centered. Will I become restless? Will I get scared and flee to daylight? But gradually my body recedes, and my thoughts grow random. Images come and go like a replay of recent events in my mind. [...] Then those images, too, fade, replaced by a jumble of memories and dreamlike scenes.[15]

It took Dr. Lilly twenty-five years to convince his fellow scientists that tanking wouldn't drive people permanently out of their minds.[16] Before his first tank trip, Lilly had thirty-five years of school and eight years of psychoanalysis.[17] He knew his mind as much as he hated his body. Hans Moravec, the roboticist from

---

12 Quoted in John Gorman, "Tanking," *OMNI Magazine,* August 1980, 62.

13 "Improvising" is how a doctor in the horror movie Amityville 3-D describes a subject's mind during a lengthy tanking experience. Richard Fleischer, dir., *Amityville 3-D,* written by David Ambrose (Orion Pictures, 1983).

14 David Itzkoff, *Mad As Hell: The Making of Network and the Fateful Vision of the Angriest Man in Movies* (New York: Times Books, 2014), 200.

15 Gorman, "Tanking," 62.

16 Ibid.

17 David Jay Brown, "From Here to Alterity and Beyond with John C. Lilly," in *Mavericks of the Mind: Conversations for the New Millennium,* eds. David Jay Brown and Rebecca McClen Novick (Berkeley: The Crossing Press, 1993), 207.

chapter three, is not so convinced of these extra-bodily journeys. He writes,

> humans need a sense of body. After twelve hours in a sensory-deprivation tank, floating in a totally dark, quiet, contactless, odorless, tasteless, body-temperature saline solution, a person begins to hallucinate, as the mind, like a television displaying snow on an empty channel, turns up the amplification in search of a signal, becoming ever less discriminating in the interpretations it makes of random sensory hiss. To remain sane, a transplanted mind will require a consistent sensory and motor image, derived from a body or from a simulation. Transplanted human minds will often be without physical bodies, but hardly ever without the illusion of having them.[18]

Dr. Lilly wasn't satisfied with just not having a body though. He experimented with substances that would push his mind as far out of it as possible. He finally settled on what he called "Vitamin K," ketamine.[19]

Memories of the Future[20]

Ketamine is classified as a "dissociative anesthetic."[21] If floating in a tank that stifles one's senses didn't already divide them, ketamine forces a chemical wedge between the mind and the body. Dr. Ralph Metzner met with Dr. Lilly many times in the

---

18 Hans Moravec, "The Senses Have No Future," in *The Virtual Dimension: Architecture, Representation, and Crash Culture,* ed. John Beckmann (New York: Princeton Architectural Press, 1998), 93.

19 See Gorman, "Tanking," 62.

20 This was Erich von Däniken's original title for his classic book, *Chariots of the Gods.* See Erich von Däniken, *Chariots of the Gods* (New York: Berkeley Books, 1999), viii.

21 Ralph Metzner, "John Lilly and Ketamine: Some Personal Recollections," in *The Ketamine Papers: Science, Therapy, and Transformation,* eds. Phil Wolfson and Glenn Hertelius (San Jose: Multidisciplinary Association for Psychedelic Studies, 2016), 48.

1960s, 1970s, and 1980s and followed his experiments closely. He writes that "ketamine expanded my consciousness into an abstract realm of thoughts and images, but without any of the sensory fireworks of the classic psychedelics and without their potential for dramatic emotional upheavals."[22] According to a mutual friend of Lilly's and Metzner's, Dr. Lilly preferred the out-of-body states that ketamine afforded because his "puritanical parents" had taught him to hate his own body. Lilly himself described the condemnation of his early autoerotic experiences. The seeds for bodily escape were planted early in the Young Lilly, and they never ceased to bloom. At one point, Metzner was told by an emergency physician who worked with Dr. Lilly that Lilly was using ketamine multiple times a day: "he told me that John claimed he was 'channeling' extraterrestrial and extra-dimensional entities — but also occasionally the evening news."[23] The physician cut all contact with Lilly at this point. Lilly claimed to have had "encounters with super-human beings who told me to go back and learn what it means to be human."[24]

Another close friend of Dr. Lilly's and fellow "ketamaniac," the video-artist known as Brummbear described the dangers of the drug during his talk at Lily's memorial: "taking ketamine is not just a flirt with death — it's a tantric fuck with death — all nine holes of your body participating — and it's not free!"[25] He goes on to say that the eventual price of the trip is your mind. Dr. Lilly was described by his peers as both playful and profound. With his wild eccentricities and soaring intellect, he annoyed as often as he enlightened. "The mind is not operating with cells alone," he told Karl Jansen.[26] "It operates with subatomic particles. If I reduce my consciousness to the Planck length of 6.624×10^{-27}, I can go anywhere in the Universe."

---

22 Ibid.

23 Ibid.

24 Quoted in Karl Jansen, *Ketamine: Dreams and Realities* (San Jose: MAPS, 2001), 65.

25 Quoted in Metzner, "John Lilly and Ketamine," 49.

26 Quoted in Jansen, *Ketamine,* 65.

We have used metaphors and metonymies of the most advanced technologies and scientific phenomenon to explain consciousness as far back as the Greek philosophers, but the technology of their time, needing constant human intervention, offered little in the way of models for the mind.[27] Since then, we have compared cognition to the machinations of the clock, the steam engine, the radio, the radar, and the computer.[28] As Dr. Lilly hints at above, the latest metaphor lies in the deep mysteries of quantum mechanics.

Anyone who claims to understand the mind is mistaken. Anyone who says they understand quantum mechanics is lying. It's not just a lack of understanding that unites the two, but our trying to define the most complex and confounding areas of our existence. Just as Robert Fludd's god-sound remained at the poetic level of application, so too do the unknowable mechanics of the subatomic world. "There is no quantum world," the physicist Niels Bohr once declared. "There is only an abstract quantum physical description."[29] Our language outreaches our understanding, but it sets us on the path. We need a vocabulary first. Bohr continues, "it is wrong to think that the task of physics is to find out how nature is. Physics concerns what we can say

27 See George Lakoff, "The Contemporary Theory of Metaphor," in *Metaphor and Thought,* ed. Andrew Ortony (Cambridge: Cambridge University Press, 1993), 202–51; Gerald Raunig, *A Thousand Machines: A Concise Philosophy of the Machine as Social Movement,* trans. Aileen Derieg (New York: Semiotext(e), 2010); and Anthony Wilden, *System and Structure: Essays in Communication and Exchange* (New York: Tavistock, 1972).

28 See Simon Penny, *Making Sense: Cognition, Computing, Art, and Embodiment* (Cambridge: MIT Press, 2017), and P.A. Vroon, "Man-Machine Analogs and Theoretical Mainstreams in Psychology," in *Current Issues in Theoretical Psychology: Selected and Edited Proceedings of the Founding Conference of the International Society for Theoretical Psychology,* eds. W.J. Baker et al. (Amsterdam: Elsevier, 1987), 393–414.

29 Quoted in Karen Barad, *Meeting the Universe Halfway: Quantum Physics and the Entanglement of Matter and Meaning* (Durham: Duke University Press, 2007), 254. See also Aage Petersen, "The Philosophy of Niels Bohr," *Bulletin of the Atomic Scientists* 19, no. 7 (1963): 8–14.

Fig. 12. Playing roulette with reality: Emily and the quantum chaos of *Coherence,* 2013. By kind permission of Alyssa Byrkit at Bella Nova Films.

about Nature."[30] What about when we can't describe it or agree on a description of it?

The 2013 film *Coherence,* written and directed by James Ward Byrkit, depicts a dinner party that devolves into quantum weirdness and suspicion after a comet passes closely by overhead. The eight dinner guests meet multiple versions of themselves, get swapped and mixed between houses, and distrust each other in rotating cliques, all due to a comet-induced split of realities and quantum decoherence. Frustrated by the reality roulette, the lead character, Em (played by Emily Foxler), goes so far as to peek into other houses to see how the night is playing out among her and her friends' other selves, eventually attempting to replace herself in a different reality of her choice. Incidentally, just like Sam Bell in *Moon,* Em is finally confronted by her other self as a voice on the phone. A minor concern in the film is the presence of a vial of ketamine.

"You can drop it into some water, just to take the edge off," Beth (played by Elizabeth Gracen) suggests. "I don't know, I'm offering. It's not medication. It has passionflower, a little valerian, and a little… ketamine." She hesitates to reveal the K, and Mike (played by Nicholas Brendon), one of the other guests,

---

30 Ibid., 13.

immediately responds, "that's a horse tranquilizer!" Beth adds, "yeah, but it's just a *whisper* of ketamine."[31] This dinner party doesn't travel "anywhere in the Universe." Indeed, its members barely leave the house, but they do experience some new possibilities. They attempt to keep it all straight with randomly numbered photographs, colored glowsticks, and totems, such as a ping pong paddle. The mere mention of ketamine is enough to unground at least one of them, wandering off into other quantum lives.

Skepticism like Mike's remains the prevailing attitude toward consciousness-expanding and mind-altering substances, but proponents of their use swear by them. Any boost beyond this state is a welcome advance. As Mark Pilkington reminds us, "we would all do well, however, to listen to Dr. Lilly's '11th Commandment', put forward in *The Deep Self* (1977): 'Thou shalt not bore god or he will destroy your universe.'"[32]

---

31 Writer and director James Ward Byrkit tells me [spoilers follow], "the *whisper* is what makes the concoction dangerous/mysterious/potent/magical/useful. But she had to say it that way to make it sound like it was also safe and recreational. We wanted the ketamine to serve double duty — one, to provide a possible explanation of the strange communal meltdown that was occurring at the party (and pulling everyone into the kitchen so that Hugh and Amir could be alone in the living room and escape with the box), and two, as a way for Em to knock herself out without killing herself." Email with the author, October 4, 2021.

32 Mark Pilkington, "In the Province of the Mind," *Frieze Magazine,* June–August 2018, https://www.frieze.com/article/what-was-inspiration-paddy-chayefskys-hallucinatory-novel. See John C. Lilly, *The Deep Self: Profound Relaxation and the Tank Isolation Technique* (New York: Simon and Schuster, 1977).

6

Death

The End of an Error

"We cannot understand and fight evil as long as we consider it to be an abstract concept external to ourselves."

— Lars Svendsen, *A Philosophy of Evil*[1]

"Fatality is the hermeticism of cause and effect. In fatality, everything you do, whatever you do, always leads to a certain end, and ultimately to the end — though that end, or the means to that end, remain shrouded in obscurity."

— Eugene Thacker, *Cosmic Pessimism*[2]

"And I find it kinda funny
I find it kinda sad
The dreams in which I'm dying
Are the best I've ever had."

— Tears for Fears, "Mad World"[3]

---

1   Lars Svendsen, *A Philosophy of Evil* (Champaign: Dalkey Archive, 2010), 231.

2   Eugene Thacker, *Cosmic Pessimism* (Minneapolis: Univocal Publishing, 2015), 14.

3   Tears for Fears, "Mad World," on *The Hurting* [LP] (New York: Mercury Records, 1983).

"The trouble with Lilly is that he is in love with death,"[4] said one of Dr. John Lilly's neuroscientist friends. Prior to diving into the depths of inner space with Lilly and *Altered States,* Paddy Chayefsky wrote *Network,* the movie he's probably best known for. Even if you know nothing about it, you might know that newsman Howard Beale was mad as hell, and he wasn't going to take it anymore! This 1976 satire of network news has lost a lot of its bite over the years due to its prescience of television programming in the meantime, but the following exchange during a pitch meeting still has teeth:

<pre>
                MAX
We could make a series out of it.
Suicide of the Week. Hell, why
limit ourselves? Execution of the
Week -- the Madame Defarge Show!
very Sunday night, bring your
knitting and watch somebody get
guillotined, hung, electrocuted,
gassed. For a logo, we'll have
some brute with a black hood over
his head. Think of the spin-offs
-- Rape of the Week --

               HOWARD
          (beginning to get
          caught up in the idea)
Terrorist of the Week?

                MAX
Beautiful!

               HOWARD
How about Coliseum '74? Every
</pre>

---

4   Quoted in Judith Hooper, "Interview: John Lilly," OMNI *Magazine,* January 1983, 58.

```
week we throw some Christians
to the lions! --

          MAX
Fantastic! The Death Hour! I
love it! Suicides, assassinations,
mad bombers, Mafia hitmen, murder
in the barbershop, human sacrifices
in witches' covens, automobile
smashups. The Death Hour! A
great Sunday night show for the
whole family. We'll wipe fucking
Disney right off the air --⁵
```

Human culture has been deeply interested in murder and the macabre since ancient ghost stories and monster tales. From the late-1960s to the early 1980s, the serial killer craze raged with headline after headline from the Manson Family in Hollywood to Ted Bundy in Washington State, from John Wayne Gacy in Chicago to the Atlanta Child Murders. "Serial killers are a phenomenon almost no one understands," writes Dr. Joel Norris. "The killer rarely fits a single stereotype, his crimes are so 'unreasonable' because the motive is internal, not explicit, and he is motivated by animal lust. Therefore, the serial killer's crimes always seem incomprehensible to reasonable people."[6] Stuck in some formative, Freudian stage of fucked, serial killers are linked by their pathologies more than their beliefs, with appetites as insatiable as their fans. As Henry Lee Lucas put it, "ain't never going to be a shortage of necks and knives."[7]

From Dahmer and *Dexter* to Hannibal Lector and *Hannibal,* we've made celebrities of serial killers and created charac-

5 Sidney Lumet, dir., *Network,* written by Paddy Chayefsky (Metro-Golden-Mayer, 1976).

6 Joel Norris, *Henry Lee Lucas: The Shocking True Story of America's Most Notorious Serial Killer* (New York: Zebra, 1991), 270–71.

7 Quoted in Ryan Green, *Trust Me: The True Story of Confession Killer Henry Lee Lucas* (independently published, 2019), 63.

ters based on them. With the recent release of Lars von Trier's *The House That Jack Built* (2018), which can be seen as a much longer, artier version of Mary Harron and Guinevere Turner's adaptation of Bret Easton Ellis's *American Psycho* (2000), and Joe Berlinger's Ted Bundy-inspired *Extremely Wicked, Shockingly Evil, and Vile* (2019), our fascination with the phenomenon doesn't seem to be waning any time soon. The song "Night Shift" by Siouxsie and the Banshees sums it up nicely: "fuck the mothers, kill the others / Fuck the others, kill the mothers / I'll put it out of my mind because… / I'm out of my mind with you / In heaven and hell with you…"[8] Any guilt we might have had becomes outrage as we scapegoat these killers with our latent murderous desires.[9]

"Running amok is a way of re-establishing one's reputation as a man to be feared and respected," writes Franco "Bifo" Berardi in his book *Heroes: Mass Murder and Suicide,* "but is also a way of escaping the world when life has become intolerable, and generally culminates in suicide."[10] We romanticize both aspects of this killing instinct, the nihilistic power-grab and the ultimate escape. It's a middle finger to everyone near and far, a fuck-the-world on both the grandest and the most intimate scales. The body is both actor and enemy. If the flesh is their god, they are devoted to destroying it. Berardi continues, "when running amok, the borders between one's body and the surrounding universe are blurred, and so is the limit between killing and being killed."[11]

---

8   Siouxsie and the Banshees, "Night Shift," on *Juju* [LP] (London: Polydor, 1981).

9   See Gary J. Shipley, "Visceral Incredulity, or Serial Killing as Necessary Anathema," in *Serial Killing: A Philosophical Anthology,* eds. Edia Connole and Gary J. Shipley (London: Schism, 2015), 21–37.

10   Franco "Bifo" Berardi, *Heroes: Mass Murder and Suicide* (New York: Verso, 2015), 55.

11   Ibid., 56.

The Streetcleaner

The Siouxsie and the Banshees song quoted above is about Peter Sutcliffe, a.k.a. The Yorkshire Ripper, who terrorized the streets of England between 1975 and 1980. Mere weeks before he was arrested, Sutcliffe sent a poem to the *Sheffield Star* newspaper called "Clueless," a poem he signed "The Streetcleaner."[12] The poem is one of many sources Justin Broadrick references as possible inspiration for the name of the first Godflesh record. Sutcliffe adopted the name because he believed he was cleaning the streets of sin.

"My desire to kill prostitutes was getting stronger than ever and it took me over completely," he said after confessing his twelfth murder.[13] "I was in a dilemma I wanted to tell someone what I was doing but I thought about how it would affect my wife and family. I wasn't too much bothered for myself." He also described his mission to cleanse the streets of prostitution as God-given: "I'd been told what my mission was, like a soldier in a war. I couldn't disobey my orders. They came from the highest authority."[14] Sutcliffe went so far as to use the unorthodox legal defense "diminished responsibility on theological grounds."[15] One of the many books about Sutcliffe is called *Voices from an Evil God,* and he believed in his divine guidance. "God invested me with the means of killing," he said. "He has got me out of trouble, and I am in God's hands."[16]

Sutcliffe started his six-year mission eliminating sex workers he saw sullying the streets of England in Leeds, Bradford, and Wakefield. Before he was caught, he became less discerning,

---

12 See Nicole Ward Jouve, *"The Streetcleaner": The Yorkshire Ripper Case on Trial* (London: Marion Boyars, 1986), 214.

13 Quoted in Barbara Jones, *Voices from an Evil God: The True Story of the Yorkshire Ripper and the Woman Who Loved Him* (London: Blake Publishing, 1993), 2–4.

14 Statement to Dr. Milne, read out in court during his trial. Quoted in "The Trial, Week Two," *The Yorkshire Ripper,* http://www.execulink.com/~kbrannen/trial04.htm.

15 Ibid.

16 Ibid.

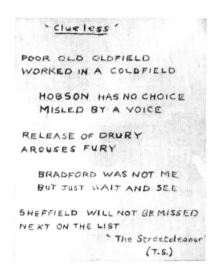

'Clueless'

POOR OLD OLDFIELD
WORKED IN A COLDFIELD

HOBSON HAS NO CHOICE
MISLED BY A VOICE

RELEASE OF DRURY
AROUSES FURY

BRADFORD WAS NOT ME
BUT JUST WAIT AND SEE

SHEFFIELD WILL NOT BE MISSED
NEXT ON THE LIST
'The Streetcleaner'
(T.S.)

Fig. 13. Signed, "The Streetcleaner."

killing seemingly at random: a university student, a 16-year-old shop girl, a 19-year-old building clerk. The largest manhunt in British law-enforcement history followed. He was ultimately found guilty of murdering thirteen women and the attempts of seven more.[17]

While I was writing this book, on November 13, 2020, Peter Sutcliffe died after refusing treatment for the COVID-19 virus.

The Hoax of Death

Where Peter Sutcliffe claimed that he heard the voice of God tell him to kill women, Henry Lee Lucas said he acted of his own volition. At the beginning of the title track of Godflesh's *Street-cleaner,* there's a voice that says, "I didn't hear voices. It was a conscious decision on my part. With me it was more of a power

---

17 See Roger Cross, *The Yorkshire Ripper: The In-Depth Study of a Mass Killer and His Methods* (London: HarperCollins UK, 1981), 144.

thing because of my fantasies, I simply acted on my fantasies."[18] It's allegedly a clip from the hours of recordings of Lucas's confessions, who was either America's most prolific serial killer or its biggest troll.

Lucas's mother was a sex worker, and he often witnessed her practicing the trade in their small home in the Virginia hill country. Growing up around these activities has been evidence to not only Lucas's sexual deviance but also his hatred of sex workers in particular, hatred of women in general, and his many murders thereof. He once described a sickness overtaking his body as a boy: "I didn't know anything happening around me. I couldn't hear, really. It was like being in a different world. I used to float through the air when I was a kid, too. I used to be layin' in bed, just felt like you're floatin' right off the bed up in the air. Just feel like I could fly. It's not a nice feeling. It's a weird feeling."[19]

Once his body was locked down, Lucas set out manipulating those around him. Prison provides the stability and control that serial killers often lack on the outside, without externally imposed structure. As Dr. Joel Norris puts it, the institution becomes their "personality skeleton."[20] Where the body is seen as a prison, here is the inverse: prison seen as the body.

Henry Lee Lucas became a cold-case clearinghouse as thousands of police officers, eager to close cases, came from all over the country to talk to him. Ex-Texas Ranger and Williamson County Sheriff Jim Boutwell and officer Bob Prince set up a task force to coordinate interviews and confessions in exchange for strawberry milkshakes, black coffee, and Pall Malls, the nonstop attention notwithstanding. Lucas leveraged the power of telling the lies everyone wants to believe. With the media as hungry for serial-killer stories to splash on their front pages as law en-

---

18 Godflesh, *Streetcleaner*. See also René Walczak, "Godflesh: Strength Through Purity," *Propaganda Magazine* 19 (Fall 1992): 40.

19 Quoted in Norris, *Henry Lee Lucas*, 40–41.

20 Ibid., 301.

Fig. 14. "Hole in the Head" by Henry Lee Lucas, colored pencil on cardstock, 2000. Courtesy of Graveface Museum.

forcement was to clear murder cases off their growing dockets, Boutwell and Lucas became a team: the Cop and the Conman.

One of Lucas's many confabulations was a child-abducting, cannibalistic cult called "The Hand of Death." Feeding off the Satanic panic of the 1980s, during which metal bands were dragged into court for inciting murder and suicide with their lyrics,[21] he and his erstwhile road partner, Ottis Toole supposedly did evil deeds, conducted business, and attended Black Masses in the name of this shadow organization, driven by "the demonic force of the universe": "what I seen with my own eyes, nobody's ever seen before. I seen the power of evil at work in the world, and I felt it practiced through me. I came to believe that my own destiny was with the power of evil. It made me do things that today I wish I could undo, but I can't. I have to pay for what I done and confess what I done."[22]

His friend and pastor in the Texas jail, Sister Clemmie, seeing only a sweet, tender man who enjoyed painting and studying the Bible with her, was convinced of his demonic possession. "Being in the middle, as it were," Eugene Thacker writes, "the demon brings together the highest and the lowest, transforming the human into a beast, and the beast into a god. The demon's metaphysical principle is 'meat.'"[23] The visceral vessel we inhabit, the body, is made of meat.

Confounding his legal counsel, Lucas was resolved to die at the hand of the state. After he killed his one true love, he sought nothing more than "salvation in his own death."[24] This rationale was his justification for confessing to murders he hadn't committed. If he killed himself, he wouldn't be allowed to join Becky in heaven. If the state killed him, he'd be with her forever after. Lucas claims that a light came into the tiny Montague County jail cell that held him captive, urging him to confess his sins. "If you confess your sins to man, I will forgive you."[25] Once con-

21 See, for instance, Mike Sager, "Fact: Five Out of Five Kids Who Murder Love Slayer," in *Revenge of the Donut Boys* (New York: Thunder's Mouth Press, 2007), 103–20.
22 Quoted in Norris, *Henry Lee Lucas*, 99–100.
23 Eugene Thacker, *In the Dust of This Planet: Horror of Philosophy, Volume 1* (Winchester: Zero Books, 2011), 116.
24 Norris, *Henry Lee Lucas*, 281. Berardi describes the killers at Columbine as motivated by similar forces: "suffering people who committed mass murder with the intention of being killed in order to be released from the intolerable burden of their life." Berardi, *Heroes*, 95.
25 Ibid., 205, 251.

victed of one murder, he toured the country confessing to multiple murders at every stop. He claimed God told him to, that it would be his path back out of the darkness.

While he seemed like law enforcement's best friend, but he was really benefiting other murderers. Though the number varied wildly, Lucas claimed as many as 600 victims, but there were only three that had evidence beyond his confessions: his mom, his girlfriend Becky Powell, and his 82-year-old landlord in Texas, Kate Rich. The Texas Rangers attributed 200 different murders to him. In the intervening years, only twenty of those have been ever passed on to other perpetrators.

In 1998, then-governor George W. Bush commuted Lucas's one death sentence to a life term. He died in prison on March 12, 2001.

It's not to say that serial killing is strictly a part of the past, but cellphones, surveillance technology, and DNA evidence have put a damper on the phenomenon. Serial killing is longitudinal, targeting individual bodies over time. However, in the twenty-first century, mass murder has supplanted the serial killing of multiple single victims. One is breadth, the other depth. Serial killers amass bodies one by one, meticulously marking each one. Mass murders make their impact all at once, like a bomb exploding. Given technological advances that include everyone with a phone as a potential Zapruder, a mass killer goes in not expecting to get away with it, usually not even expecting to survive. A mass killer goes in to take out as many bodies as possible in one go, including their own. The stakes are different, and so are the tools.

The fact that Peter Sutcliffe and Henry Lee Lucas targeted sex workers is significant — not only because both killers felt like they were preforming a service for society, but also because in their trade, sex workers use their bodies. In selling flesh, their presence and practices highlight the value of fulfilling fleshly deeds and the weaknesses of bodily desires. We are all fragile and frail.

Hostile Gospel

"Do you ever feel like there's a thousand people locked inside of you?"[26] Boxer Santeros (played by Dwayne Johnson) asks Roland Taverner (played by Sean William Scott) in Richard Kelly's *Southland Tales* (2006). "But it's your memory that keeps them glued together, keeps all those people from fighting one another. Maybe in the end that's all we have: the memory gospel." Memory also plays an important part in Kelly's first movie, *Donnie Darko* (2001). At the height of my fandom of the film, I attended a midnight screening of the director's cut at The Egyptian Theatre in Seattle. During the trivia contest that preceded the movie, I was asked to sit out due to my long string of correct answers. The movie struck something in me at a time when I needed to be struck. As Kelly himself put it, "I think you are challenged by things that are slightly beyond your grasp."[27] It is those things obscured that make a movie like this so engaging, endearing, and enduring.

Though he's never formally acknowledged it, Kelly's Frank the Rabbit character can be interpreted as a play on the pookah legend, which Robert Anton Wilson explained as follows:

> the pookah takes many forms, but is most famous when he appears as a giant, six-foot white rabbit — which is the form most Americans know from the play and film, *Harvey*. Whatever form the pookah takes, he retains the special ability of his species, which is like that of Thoth in Egyptian legend, Coyote in Native American myth, or Hanuman the Divine Monkey in Hindu lore — he can move us from one universe, or Belief System, into another, and he likes to play games with our ideas about "reality."[28]

---

26 Richard Kelly, dir., *Southland Tales* (Universal, 2006).

27 Richard Kelly, "The Making of Southland Tales," *Southland Tales* [DVD] (Universal, 2006).

28 Robert Anton Wilson, *Cosmic Trigger, Volume II: Down to Earth* (Las Vegas: New Falcon, 1991), 29.

In his 2013 book *Look at the Bunny,* Dominic Pettman reads the rabbits in both John Steinbeck's *Of Mice and Men* (1937) and Richard Adams's *Watership Down* (1972) as pookah-like guides from the future. Skipping ahead, however, is not always a promising prospect. The Cassandra conundrum of seeing imminent catastrophe and having no one in the present believe you follows the prophet, rabbit or otherwise. The vagabond rabbits of *Watership Down* led by the frequently hysterical Fiver; Lennie, George, and Candy in *Of Mice and Men* led by a rabbit-ridden future vision; Donnie Darko led by his daylight hallucinations of Frank; and Elwood led by his imaginary Harvey are all held suspect by their peers. "The list of lapine totems, no doubt, could go on and on — which is partly my point," Pettman writes.[29] Moreover, two more rabbit holes he mentions early in the book include "the bunny plot" and "the Easter egg." The former is a nagging idea that won't leave you alone until you write it out of there, and the latter, of course, refers to the hidden treats of media: images in movies, hidden features in DVD menus, secret places on websites, etc.[30]

The iconography of *Donnie Darko* starts with Frank. Like Jason Voorhees's hockey mask or Freddy Krueger's razor-fingered glove, Frank's rabbit suit is as distinctive a symbol for a movie as there has ever been. Frank is from the future, and he mentors Donnie through the film with cryptic guidance and disjointed

---

29 Dominic Pettman, *Look at the Bunny: Totem, Taboo, Technology* (London: Zero Books, 2013), 63.

30 Pettman continues, "Indeed, the notion of the Easter egg can be employed to reflect on the nature or possibility of significant surprises in a claustrophically overcoded — thus predictable — world. A world seemingly bereft of alternatives. Perhaps we need to enact rituals designed to encourage the magic bunny to break the tedious cultural algorithms that restrict every day — in the West at least — to a smooth series of anticipated rhythms. (After all, a predictable consumer is a docile and productive citizen.) Perhaps we should be finding inspiration from the temporal tricks of this particular totem to get access not to the material Easter eggs of fetishized commodities, but the hidden, virtual gift of the 'something else': an unprecedented experience, a unimagined possibility, an unanticipated alliance, and so on." Ibid.

Fig. 15. The Frank the Rabbit mask, as sketched by Richard Kelly.

advice. The setting and surroundings of Halloween, as well as the late-night bike-ride nod to *E.T.* (1982), are also endemic to this movie. Unlike any other night of the year, Halloween holds unprecedented adolescent freedoms and fears, all hidden behind masks and costumes. For example, take the music video for "What's a Girl to Do?" by Bat for Lashes.[31] Directed by Dougal Wilson in one long take, the video depicts singer Natasha Kahn joined by a group of masked youth, performing synchronized maneuvers on BMX bicycles. Aside from one of the riders wearing a rabbit mask, nothing here directly refers to the movie, but the cumulative homage is obvious. The imagery merges the dark side of Halloween's devilish allure with overwhelming temporal tensions.

Like the February 7, 1997 episode of the TV series *Millennium* in which Frank Black believes that an apocalyptic force is motivating a serial killer, in the midst of the musings of a confused, possibly schizophrenic teenage boy, *Donnie Darko* puts no less than the future of humanity at stake. Drawing from Graham Greene's "The Destructors" (1954), Adams's *Watership Down* (1972; the inspiration for Frank, according to Kelly), and Martin Scorsese's *The Last Temptation of Christ* (1988), he car-

---

31 Dougal Wilson, dir, "What's a Girl to Do?," performed by Bat for Lashes, https://vimeo.com/202203272.

ries us to the absolute brink on All Hallow's Eve. The meaning of all of this is never fully explained, but whatever it means remains important to us. It's not enough to just like the characters and to wonder. We have to care. As Stephen Jay Gould once put it, "but we also need the possibility of cataclysm, so that, when situations seem hopeless, and beyond the power of any natural force to amend, we may still anticipate salvation from a messiah, a conquering hero, a *deus ex machina,* or some other agent with power to fracture the unsupportable and institute the unobtainable."[32] The official story consists of a rogue alternate universe that must be resolved through a comic-book logic involving Donnie's death, the Manipulated Living, the Manipulated Dead, The Living Receiver, and others, all explained in character Roberta Sparrow's book, *The Philosophy of Time Travel.* Many minds and bodies are manipulated by a force from the future, but Donnie's body, crushed by an errant airplane engine, is the sacrifice required to save the world from doom.

When Richard Kelly's equally apocalyptic *Donnie Darko* follow-up, *Southland Tales,* finally hit DVD in 2008, I rented it and watched it six times over the five-day rental. Like *Donnie Darko,* this is another absurdist eschatological fairy tale, albeit on a much grander scale, with a Pynchon-esque sprawl and a large focus on politics. Where *Donnie Darko* shows remarkable restraint whenever the plot threatens to spiral out of control, *Southland Tales* just pushes that much further, reveling in its own chaos and spectacle. It's a carnival, a war, an end to humanity, a social comment, a political satire, a science fiction romp, and a laugh-out-loud comedy. It bends and blends genres so much as to be "as radical as reality itself," to borrow a phrase from several sources.[33]

The full story spills over from the film into three prequel graphic novels and borrows liberally from The Book of Revela-

---

32 Stephen Jay Gould, *Questioning the Millennium: A Rationalist's Guide to a Precisely Arbitrary Countdown* (New York: Crown, 1999), 58.

33 For one, see Steven Shaviro, *Post-Cinematic Affect* (Winchester: Zero Books, 2010), 92.

tion, Robert Frost's "The Road Not Taken" (1916), Jane's Addiction's "Three Days" (1990), T.S. Eliot's "The Hollow Men" (1925), Robert Aldrich's *Kiss Me Deadly* (1955), Alex Cox's *Repo Man* (1984), the writings of Karl Marx, and many other sources. The full scope of the story is ridiculously vast. Richard Kelly explained at the time, "I spent the last four years of my life devoted to this insane tapestry of Armageddon"; exhausted from holding it all together, he adds that this was about "getting the apocalypse out of my system once and for all."[34]

The centerpiece of this "insane tapestry of Armageddon" is a drug-induced music video sequence featuring Iraq veteran Pilot Abilene (played by Justin Timberlake) performing "All These Things That I've Done" by The Killers. Like the rest of the movie, it's over-the-top delirious, but its delirium eventually disintegrates into head-hanging melancholy and the beginning of Part VI, "Wave of Mutilation," the final act, motivated by the motif of "friendly fire" and self-destruction. Absurdity is the rule here, not the exception. In one scene, just after stopping him from committing suicide, Roland Taverner makes Martin Kefauver (played by Lou Taylor Pucci) put on his seatbelt.

Some lines seem to come from out of nowhere but form a part of Southland Tales's heavily self-conscious irony. For example, after "officer" Bart Bookman (played by Jon Lovitz) guns down two performance artists he utters, "flow my tears," quoting the title of Philip K. Dick's 1974 novel *Flow My Tears, the Policeman Said,* which offers another fleeting key to the whole apocalyptic mess.[35] On the side of his police cruiser is the Latin phrase *oderint dum metuant,* "let them hate, so long as they fear,"[36] which was a favorite saying of the Roman Emperor Caligula, a

---

34 Kelly, *Southland Tales.*

35 In addition, Roland and Ronald Taverner share a surname with the protagonist in Dick's novel. See Philip K Dick, *Flow My Tears, the Policeman Said* (New York: Doubleday, 1974).

36 Lucius Accius, "Atreus," *Archive of Performances of Greek & Roman Drama, 140–86 BCE,* http://www.apgrd.ox.ac.uk/ancient-performance/performance/809.

line that also reads like a Godflesh lyric. These are only a few examples of the film's many references and absurdities.

The plot turns on a rift in the space-time continuum in the desert near Lake Meade, through which Santaros and Taverner have traveled, doubling their physical bodies in the same timeline. Santaros's double only made it through as a burned corpse, but Taverner retained a twin. Roland and Ronald Taverner's physical bodies finally meet in an apocalyptic handshake. Their deaths are the world's death, ending it with a bang, not a whimper.

Rabbits are chosen as characters in stories because of their agility as tricksters as well as their status as prey.[37] They're able to cheat death for a time, but death always wins in the end. Death is a hunter that always gets its prey, even where humans are concerned. Justin Broadrick says, "I'm forever getting overwhelming messages from people saying, 'you saved my life.' It's brutal because I feel like I'm saving my own fucking life through this media."[38] Whether creating or destroying, we all wear the masks of death. We are perhaps most human when we're not here at all.

---

37 Pettman, *Look at the Bunny,* and Susan E. Davis and Margo Demello, *Stories Rabbits Tell* (New York: Lantern Books, 2003), 173.

38 Quoted in Antonio Poscic, "Out Demons Out," *The Wire,* April 2022, 33.

7

End
Don't Believe the Hope

"The human race sucks. Human nature is smothered out by society, job, and work and school. Instincts are deleted by laws. I see people say things that contradict themselves, or people that don't take any advantage to the gift of human life. They waste their minds on memorizing the stats of every college basketball player or how many words should be in a report when they should be using their brain on more important things. The human race isn't worth fighting for anymore."
— Eric Harris, journal entry, May 6, 1998[1]

"These premonitions of disaster remained with me. During my first days at home, I spent all my time on the veranda, watching the traffic move along the motorway, determined to spot the first signs of this end of the world by automobile, for which the accident had been my own private rehearsal."
— James in J.G. Ballard, *Crash*[2]

1

4

1   Peter Langman, ed., "Eric Harris's Journal," *School Shooters.info,* https://schoolshooters.info/sites/default/files/harris_journal_1.3.pdf.
2   J.G. Ballard, *Crash: A Novel* (London: Jonathan Cape, [1973] 1985), 50.

"Through fiction we saw the birth
Of futures yet to come
Yet in fiction lay the bones, ugly in their nakedness
Yet under this mortal sun, we cannot hide ourselves."

— Isis, "In Fiction"[3]

"My first love was science fiction films and the music that went along with them," Justin Broadrick says. "My next love was horror movies, and I became fixated with the brutal, dark, and brooding sounds that went along with those as well."[4] Godflesh's 2014 reunion record, their first release in over a decade, is called *A World Lit Only by Fire*. The title evokes a flaming planet, nations and nature scorched in ruin. It's actually a reference to a book by the same name by William Manchester about the darkness of the Middle Ages.[5] Both visions work well for Godflesh's sound: it's dark, brutal, and could have come from a tumultuous past or a post-apocalyptic future. The hard, cold sound could be bones or stones as easily as it could be bricks or concrete blocks.

"Have you ever participated in genocide?" was the question on one of the forms Broadrick filled out on his first trip to the States after 9/11. "I always said Godflesh was, to some extent, protest music. It comes from an anarcho-punk background." Then, echoing Columbine High School gunman Eric Harris above, he adds, "but after all the idealistic sloganeering and stuff, I sort of went the opposite way. I started to feel like the human race wasn't worth saving after all."[6] As he sings on "Life Giver Life Taker" from *A World Lit Only by Fire,* "the dying sun / Is all ours / It will reclaim / Our fallen earth."[7]

---

3   Isis, "In Fiction," on *Panopticon* [LP] (Los Angeles: Ipecac Records, 2012).

4   Quoted in Garth Ferrante, "Godflesh Explains 'Selfless''s Song Titles," *Godflesh.com,* August 1994, https://godflesh.com/articles/int2.txt.

5   See William Manchester, *A World Lit Only by Fire: The Medieval Mind and the Renaissance: Portrait of an Age* (New York: Little, Brown & Co., 1992).

6   Quoted in Jason Heller, "Justin Broadrick of Jesu," *AV Club,* April 5, 2007, https://film.avclub.com/justin-broadrick-of-jesu-1798211103.

7   Godflesh, "Life Giver Life Taker," on *A World Lit Only by Fire* [LP] (London: Avalanche Recordings, 2014).

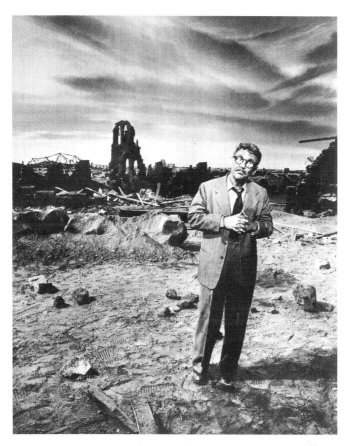

Fig. 16. Burgess Meredith in *The Twilight Zone,* 1959.

Future-minded science-fiction writers have recently been comparing the dearth of mentions of the twenty-second century so far in the twenty-first to the many mentions of the twenty-first at the same point last century.[8] It is as if we can't even im-

8   See Abraham Riesman, "William Gibson Has a Theory About Our Cultural Obsession with Dystopias," *Vulture,* August 1, 2017, https://www.vulture.com/2017/08/william-gibson-archangel-apocalypses-dystopias.html, and

agine our future anymore, but dystopic doom was around back then, too. "I abhor humanity," Birkin says to Ursula in D.H. Lawrence's 1920 novel, *Women in Love,* "I wish it was swept away. It could go, and there would be no absolute loss, if every human being perished tomorrow. The reality would be untouched. Nay, it would be better."[9] I distinctly remember an episode of *The Twilight Zone* I watched as a kid. It was called "Time Enough at Last" and starred the late Burgess Meredith. I don't remember all of it, just the end: there's a man, a bibliophile, the last person left on earth, and he's ecstatic because he's surrounded by books, mounds and mounds of them. He finally breaks his reverie in order to get started reading. Then he breaks his glasses.`

The trepidation of that tragic moment, recombinant with worries of the apocalypse, was a seed planted in my head. And more than any other Cold War-era image of imminent destruction splashed on the television during my childhood, the nerd in me nurtured that single idea, that the apocalypse seemed inevitable, and it did not look like a particularly good time. In fact, it looked like a tailor-made, personal purgatory.

Barry Brummett writes that apocalyptic orators "claim special knowledge of a hidden order, to advise others to make great sacrifices on the basis of that knowledge, even to predict specific times and place for the end of the world."[10] In spite of *The Twilight Zone* episode, I've always considered myself more concerned with my own demise than with the end of the word, but the latter is clearly hanging heavy in the mass-mind. Brummett also writes that the strategy of apocalyptic rhetoric is "to respond to a sense of chaos and anomie, whether acute or potential, with reassurances of a plan that is ordering history."[11] Between looming pandemics, postponed human holocaust, and all the other

SCI-Arc Channel, "Bruce Sterling & Benjamin Bratton in Conversation," *YouTube,* November 5, 2018, https://www.youtube.com/watch?v=Z0__x5S-G8WY.

9   D.H. Lawrence, *Women in Love* (New York: Thomas Seltzer, 1920), 143.

10   Barry Brummett, *Contemporary Apocalyptic Rhetoric* (New York: Praeger, 1991), 87.

11   Ibid.

global weirding, there are certainly those who would have us believe that our doom is imminent. As far as the darker strains of heavy metal music are concerned, we deserve the anxiety, as it's likely our own fault.

Black Metallic[12]

Black metal's corpse-paint makeup and entropic rhythms give sight and sound to the grinding ghost of human civilization. More so even than the industrial pounding of Godflesh, black metal is what's left when the systems have all broken down. Evan Calder Williams sees the ethos of the genre as "a battlefield from the start, as a phenomenal working through of that imagined site, that promised zone of contestation where the contemporary world is swept away to confront the old antagonisms."[13] The battle is with the contemporary world itself. Often thought of as Satanic from the outside, orthodox black metal is typically just anti-religion, anti-Western, and longing for Norwegian Nationalism over some horned devil as such. As Gaahl, former lead vocalist of Gorgoroth, told Peter Beste, "I think Christianity has made people afraid of solitude; afraid of the idea of being alone."[14] Theirs is a call for the Old Norse ways and solitary contemplation, a return to the time before the Westernization of Scandinavia.

At barely 30 years old, black metal is a relatively young musical genre. Its roots running back to such theatrical and thrash acts as Hellhammer, Celtic Frost, Venom, Bathory, Mercyful Fate, and Slayer, it finally found fertile ground in Scandinavia in the late 1980s and early 1990s. This second wave, including such bands as Mayhem, Darkthrone, Burzum, and Emperor, is what most are referring to when they utter the words. As author

---

12 Catherine Wheel, "Black Metallic," on *Ferment* [LP] (Los Angeles: Fontana, 1992).

13 Evan Calder Williams, *Combined and Uneven Apocalypse: Luciferian Marxism* (Winchester: Zero Books, 2011), 131.

14 Quoted in Peter Beste, *True Norwegian Black Metal: We Turn in the Night Consumed by Fire* (New York: Vice Books, 2008), 107.

Ulrike Serowy puts it, black metal is "music that touches the inmost depths, goes beyond words, music that conjures infinity."[15] The bands and fans all wear head-to-toe black leather, wrist- and armbands, boots with spikes or nails, and black and white corpse paint.

Described as "the most widely demonized and vilified music scene in rock history," black metal took traditional metal to new extremes.[16] The major characters involved in Norway's second wave include Øystein Aarseth (a.k.a Eronymous) of Mayhem, Per Yngve Ohlin (a.k.a. Dead) of Mayhem, Varg Vikernes (a.k.a. Count Grishnackh) of Burzum and Mayhem, and Bärd Eithun (a.k.a. Faust) of Emperor, among several others. "Dead's name was an ever-looming portent of his destiny" write Michael Moynihan and Didrik Søderlind in their 1998 exposé of the scene, *Lords of Chaos*.[17] Very much into self-mutilation, often on stage, Dead eventually shot himself in the head with a shotgun. His bandmate Euronymous found the body, took pictures, and reportedly took pieces of his skull and brains. One of the pictures ended up as the cover art for the live Mayhem record, *Dawn of the Black Hearts,* and Euronymous supposedly made a stew out of Dead's brains and necklaces out of pieces of his skull.

The sometime bass player for Mayhem and full-time one-man-band Burzum, Grishnackh, paranoid of an alleged plot by Euronymous to kill him, beat him to the punch. One late night in Oslo, Grishnackh stabbed Euronymous twenty-three separate times, two in the head, five in the neck, and sixteen in the back.[18] Euronymous had been the figurehead of the Norwegian black metal scene. His record store in Oslo, Helvete, had served as a central meeting place for bands and fans, as well as a place to buy records and paraphernalia. It was darkly lit, and Eurony-

---

15   Ulrike Serowy, *Skogtatt: A Novella* (Lohmar: Hablizel, 2013), 33.

16   Andrew O'Hehir, "Sympathy for the Devil Worshipers: 'Until the Light Takes Us' Movie Review," *Salon,* December 7, 2009, https://www.salon.com/2009/12/07/until_the_light/

17   Michael Moynihan and Didrik Søderlind, *Lords of Chaos: The Rise of the Satanic Metal Underground* (Port Townsend: Feral House, 1998), 58.

18   Darcey Steinke, "Satan's Cheerleaders," SPIN *Magazine,* February 1996, 66.

mous wanted it to be kept completely dark and make customers use torches to see the records and their way around.

Underwhelmed by what he saw as Euronymous's posturing without action, Grishnackh allegedly set about burning down churches. Grishnackh's philosophy is one of nationalism. He sees Christianity as colonialist, the religion having moved into Norway and displaced the native Norse religion. However, his intentions did not keep the church burnings from being seen as "Satanically motivated" by the media. The heavy metal magazine *Kerrang!* ran a cover story that read, "Arson… Death… Satanic Ritual… The Ugly Truth about Black Metal" and the spread bore the quotation, "We are but slaves of the one with horns…"[19] across the top of its pages. "Copycat church attacks followed throughout the Northern Hemisphere, often accompanied with spray-painted pentacles and 666's and so forth, and whatever had once been distinctive about the Norwegian scene just became, in Vikernes' words, "'a bunch of brain-dead, heavy-metal guys.'"[20]

The image of the black metal scene at large is one of darkness and evil. Dick Hebdige writes, "in most cases, it is the subculture's stylistic innovations which first attract the media's attention. Subsequently deviant or 'anti-social' acts — vandalism, swearing, fighting, 'animal behavior' — are 'discovered' by the police, the judiciary, the press; and these acts are used to 'explain' the subculture's original transgression of sartorial codes. In fact, either deviant behavior or the identification of a distinctive uniform (or more typically a combination of the two) can provide the catalyst for a moral panic."[21] The moral panic that followed the church burnings illustrates how easily such a scene is vilified and labeled "Satanic." Subcultures are largely imagistic and operate on the level of surfaces. Never mind that half the members of the bands involved are or were serving prison

19 *Kerrang! Magazine* 436, March 27, 1993, quoted in Moynihan and Søderlind, *Lords of Chaos,* 100–101.
20 O'Hehir, "Sympathy for the Devil Worshipers."
21 Dick Hebdige, *Subculture: The Meaning of Style* (New York: Routledge, 1979), 93.

terms for their actions. A movement as such quickly becomes regarded as exclusively stylistic. Attaching Satan to a movement that was largely nationalist in nature is a move that occurs on the surface of the phenomenon. Dayal Patterson points out that black metal "will surely continue to innovate and evolve, and this should be celebrated."[22] Once it reached the shores of the States, the bands there show how far this style has spread since its spiked-leather beginnings. In the US, where guns outnumber people and school shootings are rampant, the reception of black metal is also different. Since 2014 there has been more than one mass shooting a day on average.[23] Violent music and violent outcomes on the other side of the world are one thing. Violent music in a violent context right down the street is quite another.

A Looming Resonance[24]

In America, where history is always already lost to the self-same spectacle encroaching on Norway, black metal seeks not a return to any sort of nationalism but a return to the wilderness, to introspection, away from media and technology. Borrowing everything from the Scandinavians except the panda paint, American black metal bands blend the core aesthetic with other subgenres to great effect, the most notable and widespread being the rising and falling structures of post-rock and the ambient guitar squalls of shoegaze. All of these subgenres are about meditation, contemplation, and introspection, in sharp contrast to the pomp and posturing of their rock-and-roll forebears. Over the past several years, this melding and welding of metal has become my favorite accompanying sound for almost any activity. Its energy, its all-encompassing crests and crumbles, its sheer

---

22 Dayal Patterson, *Black Metal: The Evolution of the Cult* (Port Townsend: Feral House, 2013), 484.

23 Alvin Chang, "Every Mass Shooting in the US – A Visual Database," *The Guardian,* May 27, 2021, https://www.theguardian.com/us-news/ng-interactive/2021/may/27/us-mass-shootings-database.

24 Wolves in the Throne Room, "A Looming Resonance," on *Malevolent Grain* [EP] (Los Angeles: Southern Lord, 2009).

power moves me in ways no other genre has in many years. And I am not alone: the darkness of this stuff touches something in us, something buried deep in our beings, in our nature.

Among the best of this mix of subgenres stateside are Washington state's Wolves in the Throne Room and California's Deafheaven. The former's Cascadian black metal is as majestic as it is monolithic, and mixing the forest and the trees, their epic songs can be as dense as they are sparse. Their explanation of the draw of black metal from a 2006 interview is worth quoting at length.

True Norwegian black metal is completely unbalanced — that is why it is so compelling and powerful. It is the sound of utter torment, believing to one's core that winter is eternal. black metal is about destruction, destroying humanity; destroying one's own self in an orgy of self-loathing and hopelessness. I believe one must focus on this image of eternal winter in order to understand black metal for it is a crucial metaphor that reveals our sadness and woe as a race. In our hubris, we have rejected the earth and the wisdom of countless generations for the baubles of modernity. In return, we have been left stranded and bereft in this spiritually freezing hell.

To us, the driving impulse of black metal is more about deep ecology than anything else and can best be understood through the application of eco-psychology. Why are we sad and miserable? Because our modern culture has failed — we are all failures. The world around us has failed to sustain our humanity, our spirituality. The deep woe inside black metal is about fear — that we can never return to the mythic, pastoral world that we crave on a deep subconscious level. Black metal is also about self-loathing, for modernity has transformed us, our minds, bodies and spirit, into an alien life form; one not suited to life on earth without the mediating forces of technology, culture and organized religion. We are weak and pitiful in our strength over the earth — in conquering, we have destroyed ourselves. black metal expresses disgust with

Fig. 17. Back to Nature: Wolves in the Throne Room. Photo by Peter Beste. By kind permission of the photographer.

humanity and revels in the misery that one finds when the falseness of our lives is revealed.[25]

The urge to return to our roots is a prevailing ethos in black metal of all paints. In Norway, it's about returning to the Norse traditions that predate the Western influences on the culture there. For Wolves in the Throne Room, it's about a return to nature. "Our music is balanced in that we temper the blind rage of black metal with the transcendent truths of the universe that reveal themselves with age and experience," they continue. "Our relationship with the natural world is a healing force in our lives."[26] Drummer and one of the two brothers that make up the core of Wolves in the Throne Room, Aaron Weaver was taken by black metal upon first hearing it.

> It's more about creating a trance effect. It's really got more in common with shamanic drumming and with noise music. It's not heavy metal, it's not riffs, it's not head-banging music at all. [...] It's meditative music. Most heavy metal is very extroverted. It's about putting on a big show and head banging and drinking a beer with your buddies. Black metal is the exact opposite. It's all about gazing inwards and trying to discover things about yourself.[27]

Their music is introspective to the point of turning one inside out. "The real truth hidden in black metal is a call to completely destroy the world. [...] I'm talking about destroying the world on a spiritual level."[28]

---

25 Quoted in Bradley Smith, "Interview with Wolves in the Throne Room," *Nocturnal Cult,* 2006, http://www.nocturnalcult.com/WITTRint.htm.
26 Ibid.
27 Quoted in Matthew Moyer, "Wolves in the Throne Room: From Mount Olympia," *Ghettoblaster Magazine* 30 (Winter 2011): 42. Simon Reynolds described Godflesh's Streetcleaner as "internal exile." Simon Reynolds, "Godflesh Streetcleaner," *Melody Maker,* October 14, 1989, 37.
28 Quoted in Andrew Parks, "Wolves in the Throne Room Profile," *Decibel Magazine,* April 2009, 20.

Fig. 18. Rotten with Perfection: Sunbather-era Deafheaven. Photo by Reid Haithcock, 2013. Licensed from photographer.

Weaver discusses the connections between black metal and the radical Northwestern culture he and his brother are immersed in, both of which are about "critiquing civilization, yearning for a more ancient sense of the world, a connection with tradition and nature that we've perhaps lost as modern people."[29] Considering themselves largely apolitical, their ideology has been described as "ecoanarchism." That's not the whole of it, of course, he adds, "then the darker side of it as well exists in both worlds. In both the black metal world and the ecological punk world, a hatred of humanity and a strong sense of misanthropy as we look around and see what humanity has wrought."[30]

Where Wolves in the Throne Room want to reverse the damage done by humanity by returning to earlier times, Deafheaven withdraws further into the self. Their breakout 2013 record, *Sunbather,* describes a decidedly human situation. "The record surrounds the feeling of longing for perfection and the frustration and sadness of knowing that it can never be achieved," says

---

29 Quoted in Moyer, "Wolves in the Throne Room," 42.
30 Ibid. See also Timothy Morton, "At the Edge of the Smoking Pool of Death: Wolves in the Throne Room," in *Helvete: A Journal of Black Metal Theory Issue 1,* eds. Amelia Ishmael et al. (Brooklyn: punctum books, 2013), 21–28.

vocalist George Clarke.[31]You don't have to be a perfectionist to want more from life. You just have to be human.

"You might come across American black metal and see a greater tendency to humanize the terms, which may seem somewhat contradictory," says He Who Crushes Teeth from Deafheaven's California neighbors, Bone Awl, "but I think an unknown goal in American black metal is to level the vocabulary and draw attention to the fact that nothing is outside of humanity."[32] The rhetorical critic Kenneth Burke defined the human as "the symbol using, making, and mis-using animal, inventor of the negative, separated from his natural condition by instruments of his own making, goaded by the spirit of hierarchy, and rotten with perfection."[33] The very Burkean phrase "rotten with perfection" is an apt description of *Sunbather,* not only in its intent but also in its execution. "The 'Sunbather' is essentially the idea of perfection," Clarke says, "a wealthy, beautiful, perfect existence that is naturally unattainable and the struggles of having to deal with that reality because of your own faults, relationship troubles, family troubles, death, etc."[34] Balancing ambitions for more with an appreciation for what we have is a definitively human struggle. Wanting to transcend those limits and find out what's beyond them is human as well.

31 Quoted in Jason Heller, "Deafheaven Profile," *Decibel Magazine,* August 2013, 32.
32 Quoted in Brandon Stosuy, "Meaningful Leaning Mess," in *Hideous Gnosis: Black Metal Theory Symposium 1,* ed. Nicola Masciandaro (Lexington: CreateSpace, 2012), 152.
33 Kenneth Burke, *Language as Symbolic Action: Essays on Life, Literature, and Method* (Berkeley: University of California Press, 1966), 16.
34 Quoted in Anthony Glaser, "Interview: Deafheaven," *National Underground,* March 11, 2013, http://nationalunderground.org/2013/03/11/interview-deafheaven/.

Localizing Hell

Touted by some as the "Scariest Music in the World,"[35] Stalaggh,
and later Gulaggh, went to the very home of humanity's limits
for their sounds: the asylum. The "gh" suffix in their name stands
for "global holocaust" because that's what they were trying to set
off, like some sort of a planet-spanning Helter Skelter.[36] Named
after the POW camps in Nazi Germany (Stalag) and the rehabili-
tation and labor camps in the former Soviet Union (Gulag), they
tell Brandon Stosuy of *Pitchfork,* "our name represents the total
annihilation of human life."[37] They continue,

> black metal made people burn churches and kill people and
> terrorize in the name of intolerance. Music can cause chaos
> and fear. People into gothic, ambient, electro music have an
> overall depressed and dark state of mind. They are generally
> not averse to suicide. They are into auto-mutilation. We con-
> sider this a good start, but it is only a beginning. They should
> be on all fields motivated to more radical actions, against
> both themselves and other human beings. We want people to
> feel miserable and depressed.[38]

Stalaggh and Gulaggh were made up of several unnamed
members of Dutch and Belgian black metal bands who set out to
make the most oppressive music possible topped with the vocals
of criminally insane mental patients. Screams allegedly belonging to a man who murdered his own mother by stabbing her
thirty times and to another man who committed suicide soon

---

35 See The Weirdnet, "Scariest Music in the World?," *BitChute,* November 1,
    2017, https://www.bitchute.com/video/zhsk3HVz5btd/.
36 See Jerome Reuter, "Stalaggh/Gulaggh: A Window into Suffering and the
    Necessity for Transgressive Art," *Diabolique Magazine,* November 15, 2020,
    https://diaboliquemagazine.com/stalaggh-gulaggh-a-window-into-suffer-
    ing-and-the-necessity-for-transgressive-art/.
37 Quoted in Brandon Stosuy, "Show No Mercy," *Pitchfork,* June 20, 2007,
    https://pitchfork.com/features/show-no-mercy/6633-show-no-mercy/.
38 Ibid.

Fig. 19. "Art is creative, we are destructive." Stalaggh: The faces of Global Holocaust.

after the recording was over. "We decided that a normal black metal vocalist was not what we were looking for," they say. "The pain and hate in the vocals must be real, not acted. We needed humans with a real mental illness. Only someone in constant mental pain or with a homicidal aggression could provide the vocals for our Audio-Terror."[39] The anguished howling of a human out of their mind is the pure sound of hell.

"For thousands of years human beings have tried to localize hell," Verge (played by Bruno Ganz) explains in Lars von Trier's 2018 movie *The House That Jack Built*. "Among other methods by seeking the sound it generates. One shouldn't focus on extracting screams and wailing because the cries of pain of so many millions of individuals together becomes what you have just heard: a buzzing sound whose intensity will increase

---

39 Ibid.

as we get ever closer to the presence of suffering."[40] Through his thoughts and deeds, to the afterlife of the underworld, Verge is Jack's guide, and a reference to Dante Alighieri's. Throughout the film, the titular Jack (played by Matt Dillon) is attempting to construct a house. But he is an engineer, not an architect. As to the difference: "an engineer reads music, an architect plays music," he explains to one of his victims. Jack is also a serial killer.

"The art of engineering is first and foremost about statics," he says. "That is so things remain standing in spite of the various forces that impact the buildings." Jack reduces the engineering problems of his house to the material used in its construction. "I often say that the material does the work. In other words, it has a kind of will of its own and by following it, the result will be the most exquisite." During this discussion, he mentions Adolf Hitler's architect, Albert Speer, and Speer's use of both strong and weak materials in his buildings so that a thousand years later they would leave behind "aesthetically perfect ruins."[41] Like the three little pigs, Jack tries bricks, wood, and other conventional building materials to no avail. "Find the material, Jack," Verge says, "and let it do the work."[42]

Jack stashes his victims' bodies in a large, walk-in freezer space. After every kill, he adds the body to the pile. Before the bodies become rigid in their death and frozen in their decomposition, they are malleable. After experimenting with them, like he had with brick and wood, he finds that he can twist them into new poses, pose them into new scenes. At Verge's urging, the house that Jack builds is of the frozen corpses of his many victims, frozen yet molded. The ideal building material ends up being dead people, human bodies used as raw materials for the most basic technology: shelter. All of Jack's murderous labor leads him to a portal to hell. Even as his deeds have left him no alternative, his hubris finds him still attempting to avoid dam-

---

40 Lars von Trier, dir., *The House That Jack Built* (Zentropa Entertainments, 2018).

41 Ibid.

42 Ibid.

nation's eternal flames. One imagines the whole of humanity, when the Earth will sustain us no more.

This Mortal Soil

The use of mental patients for something as frivolous as a black-metal recording or frozen bodies as building materials might send up humanitarian red flags, but as human population continues to grow, humans are more likely to be used as a resource, raw materials for any use whatever. Moreover, the human rights in question diminish as the resources grow as well. In what Broadrick calls the "constant repetition of existence,"[43] we are the mistake that keeps on mistaking, mistaking ourselves as exceptional, mistaking ourselves as unique, mistaking ourselves as important. Even when we recognize ourselves as fallible, we still make more; the crumbling façades of buildings and the crumbling flesh of bodies.

Humanity doesn't scale, and human nature is a farce. People will do what people will do, but we will rarely surprise you. That complete lack of surprise is all that could be called human nature. The sad predictability of the species is its nature. As Eugene Thacker puts it, "on the one hand we as human beings are the problem; on the other hand at the planetary level of the Earth's deep time, nothing could be more insignificant than the human."[44] Where posthumanism is most often associated with the biotechnical augmentations of cyborgs discussed before, fixing us up rather than following after we've gone, this is the posthumanism of extinction.[45]

43 Quoted in Jason Heller, "Justin Broadrick of Jesu," *AV Club,* April 5, 2007, https://film.avclub.com/justin-broadrick-of-jesu-1798211103. Douglas Coupland calls it "Strangelove Reproduction," that is, "having children to make up for the fact that one no longer believes in the future." Douglas Coupland, *Generation X: Tales for An Accelerated Culture* (New York: St. Martin's Press, 1991), 135.

44 Eugene Thacker, *In the Dust of This Planet: Horror of Philosophy, Volume 1* (Winchester: Zero Books, 2011), 158.

45 Daniel Lukes, "Black Metal Machine: Theorizing Industrial Black Metal," in *Helvete,* eds. Ishmael et al., 71–73. See also Cary Wolfe, *What is Posthu-*

In Alan Weisman's 2007 book, *The World Without Us,* which speculates what life on Earth will like after humans cease to exist, he describes us as senders rather than receivers of signals, and that radio waves dispatched and drifting through space will be our final legacy. The human brain is also a transmitter, broadcasting electric impulses at very low frequencies that some believe can be focused to exact actions at a distance. "That may seem far-fetched," Weisman writes, "but it's also a definition of prayer."[46]

On a more grounded note, David Leo Rice writes,

absurd as this hope surely is, I wonder if there might be a grain of truth in it. Since we, too, are creatures of the earth, made of earthly materials (as are our digital devices), perhaps there is something in our nature that can reach beyond our limited time as humans, and partake in the larger cycle of dust returning to dust. Perhaps some part of the consciousness of the earth itself exists within us, and will go on existing.[47]

---

manism? (Minneapolis: University of Minnesota Press, 2009), and Jussi Parikka, "Planetary Memories: After Extinction, the Imagined Future," in *After Extinction,* ed. Richard Grusin (Minneapolis: University of Minnesota Press, 2018), 27–49.

46 Alan Weisman, *The World Without Us* (New York: St. Martin's Press, 2007), 274.

47 David Leo Rice, "The Overlook Hotel," *The Believer,* October 31, 2017, https://believermag.net/logger/overlook/. He continues, "to believe this is to believe in an afterlife of time, rather than space: to believe that human consciousness, once it has become disembodied, will not travel upward or downward to heaven or hell, nor into space as radio waves, but rather that it will linger here on earth, as earth, even when that earth is transformed into a planet that, if we were to perceive it while still human, would have to be called alien. This is the dream of the entire species being present at its own funeral." As Roberts puts it, "the end is final, and yet it also represents a strange new beginning." Adam Roberts, *It's the End of the World, But What Are We Really Afraid Of?* (London: Elliott & Thompson Limited, 2020), 9. See also Timothy Morton, *Ecology without Nature: Rethinking Environmental Aesthetics* (Cambridge: Harvard University Press, 2010).

Weak transmitters, antennae for sound, or just sentient meat, how ever we seek a way beyond them, we are bound by our bodies: malleable yet mortal, elastic yet earthbound. We are soil as much as we are souls.[48] The dust of this planet is people.[49]

---

48 As William Bryant Logan writes, "human bodies belong to and depend on dirt. We spend our lives hurrying away from the real, as though it were deadly to us. But the soil is all of the earth that is really ours." William Bryant Logan, *Dirt: The Ecstatic Skin of the Earth* (New York: Riverhead, 1995), 97.

49 Like much of the rest of this book, this final line owes its existence to both McKenzie Wark and Eugene Thacker. It combines and pays homage to the last lines of Wark's *Dispositions* (Cromer: Salt Publishing, 2002) and Thacker's *In the Dust of This Planet*.

Discography

Agent Orange. *This Is the Voice* [LP]. Los Angeles: Enigma Records, 1986.

Ain, Martin Eric. "A Dying God Coming into Human Flesh." On *Monotheist* [LP]. Recorded by Celtic Frost. Dortmund: Century Media Records, 2006.

Catherine Wheel. "Black Metallic." On *Ferment* [LP]. Los Angeles: Fontana, 1992.

Deafheaven. *Infinite Granite* [LP]. Los Angeles: Sargent House 2021.

———. *New Bermuda* [LP]. Los Angeles: Anti-., 2015.

———. *Ordinary Corrupt Human Love* [LP]. Los Angeles: Anti-, 2018.

———. *Roads to Judah* [LP]. Beverly: Deathwish, Inc., 2013.

———. *Sunbather* [LP]. Beverly: Deathwish, Inc., 2013.

Fall of Because. *Life Is Easy* [CD]. Chicago: Invisible Records, 1999.

Godflesh. *A World Lit Only by Fire* [LP]. London: Avalanche Recordings, 2014.

———. *Hymns* [LP]. London: Music for Nations, 2001.

———. *Godflesh* [EP]. London: Silent Scream, 1988.

———. *Post Self* [LP]. London: Avalanche Recordings, 2017.

———. *Pure* [LP]. London: Earache Records, 1992.

———. *Selfless* [LP]. New York: Columbia, 1994.

———. *Streetcleaner* [LP]. London: Earache Records, 1989.

————. *Streetcleaner: Live at Roadburn 2011* [LP]. Roadburn Records, 2013.

Greymachine. *Disconnected* [LP]. Los Angeles: Hydra Head Records, 2009.

Gulaggh. *Vortuka* [LP]. New Era Productions, 2008.

Head of David. *Dustbowl* [LP]. London: Blast First, 1988.

————. *White Elephant* [LP]. London: Blast First, 1989.

Isis. "In Fiction." On *Panopticon* [LP]. Los Angeles: Ipecac Records, 2012.

Jesu. *Conqueror* [LP]. Los Angeles, Hydra Head Records, 2007.

————. *Heartache & Dethroned* [EP]. Los Angeles: Hydra Head Records, 2010.

————. *Jesu* [LP]. Los Angeles: Hydra Head Records, 2004.

————. *Pale Sketches* [LP]. Avalanche Recordings, 2007.

JK Flesh. *Posthuman* [LP]. 3by3 Music, 2012.

Manic Street Preachers. "Mausoleum." On *The Holy Bible* [LP]. New York: Epic Records, 1984.

Milemarker. "Insect Incest." On *Sex Jams* [7" single]. New Gretna: Bloodlink Records, 1999.

Miller, Daniel. "T.V.O.D." On *Warm Leatherette* [7" single]. Recorded by The Normal. London: Mute Records, 1978.

Napalm Death. *Scum* [LP]. London: Earache Records, 1986.

Open Mike Eagle. *Brick Body Kids Still Daydream* [LP]. Tucson: Mello Music Group, 2017.

Robbins, J. "Motorist." On *Jackpot Plus* [7" single]. Recorded by Jawbox. Washington, DC: Dischord Records, 1993.

Siouxsie and the Banshees. "Night Shift." On *Juju* [LP]. London: Polydor, 1981.

Siouxsie Sioux & Budgie. "Miss the Girl." On *Feast* [LP]. Recorded by The Creatures. London: Polydor, 1983.

Stalaggh. *Nihilistik Terror* [CD]. New Era Productions, 2006

————. *Projekt Misanthropia* [CD]. Autopsy Kitchen Records, 2007.

————. *Projekt Nihil* [LP]. New Era Productions, 2003.

————. *Projekt Terror* [LP]. Total Holocaust Records, 2004.

————. *Pure Misanthropia* [LP]. New Era Productions, 2008.

Tears for Fears. "Mad World." On *The Hurting* [LP]. New York: Mercury Records, 1983.

Wolves in the Throne Room. *Black Cascade* [LP]. Los Angeles: Southern Lord, 2009.

———. *Celestial Lineage* [LP]. Los Angeles: Southern Lord, 2011.

———. *Primordial Arcana* [LP]. Philadelphia: Relapse Records, 2021.

———. *Thrice Woven* [LP]. Olympia: Artemsia Records, 2017.

———. *Two Hunters* [LP]. Los Angeles: Southern Lord, 2007.

Filmography

Aites, Aaron, and Audrey Ewell, dirs. *Until the Light Takes Us.* Field Pictures, 2009.

Ambrose, David, and Richard Fleischer, dirs. *Amityville 3-D.* Orion Pictures, 1983.

Barron, Steve, dir. *Electric Dreams.* Written by Rusty Lemorande. Virgin Films, 1984.

Brahm, John, dir. *The Twilight Zone.* Season 1, Episode 8, "Time Enough at Last," written by Rod Sterling, starring Burgess Meredith. Aired November 20, 1959, on CBS.

Byrkit, James Ward, dir. *Coherence.* Oscilloscope Laboratories, 2013.

Cronenberg, Brandon, dir. *Possessor.* Rhombus Media, 2020.

Cronenberg, David, dir. *Crash.* Universal Pictures, 1996.

———. *Videodrome.* Alliance Communications, 1983.

Ducournau, Julia. dir. *Titane.* Kazak Productions, 2021.

Dunn, Sam, and Scott McFadyen, dirs. *Metal Evolution.* Banger Films, 2011.

Glazer, Jonathan, dir. *Under the Skin.* BFI, 2013.

Jones, Duncan, dir. *Moon.* Sony Pictures Classics, 2009.

Jonze, Spike, dir. *Her.* Annapurna Pictures, 2013.

Kelly, Richard, dir. *Donnie Darko.* Newmarket, 2001.

———. *Southland Tales.* Universal, 2006.

Lumet, Sidney, dir. *Network.* Written by Paddy Chayefsky. Metro-Golden-Mayer, 1976.

Pizzolatto, Nic. *True Detective.* HBO, 2014.

Russell, Ken, dir. *Altered States.* Warner Bros., 1980.

von Trier, Lars, dir. *The House That Jack Built.* Zentropa Entertainments, 2018.

Wilson, Dougal. dir. "What's a Girl to Do?" Performed by Bat for Lashes. https://vimeo.com/202203272.

Bibliography

Accius, Lucius. "Atreus." *Archive of Performances of Greek & Roman Drama, 140–86 BCE.* http://www.apgrd.ox.ac.uk/ancient-performance/performance/809.

Adams, Richard. *Watership Down: A Novel.* London: Rex Collings, 1972.

Alexander, Chris. "The Skin He's In." *Fangoria Magazine* 322, May 2014, 42–46.

Anselmi, J.J. *Doomed to Fail: The Incredibly Loud History of Doom, Sludge, and Post Metal.* Los Angeles: Rare Bird Books, 2020.

Balch, Robert W., and David Taylor. "Salvation in a UFO." *Psychology Today* 10, no. 5 (October 1976): 58–60.

Ballard, J.G. *Crash: A Novel.* London: Jonathan Cape, [1973] 1985.

———. *Extreme Metaphors: Collected Interviews.* Edited by Simon Sellars and Dan O'Hara. London: Fourth Estate, 2012.

———. *High-Rise: A Novel.* London: Jonathan Cape, 1975.

———. *The Atrocity Exhibition.* London: Jonathan Cape, 1970.

Barad, Karen. *Meeting the Universe Halfway: Quantum Physics and the Entanglement of Matter and Meaning.* Durham: Duke University Press, 2007.

Barker, Martin, Jane Arthors, and Ramaswami Harindranath. *The Crash Controversy: Censorship Campaigns and Film Reception.* London: Wallflower Press, 2001.

Bartkewitcz, Anthony. "Vision: Escape: Justin Broadrick." *Decibel Magazine,* March 2007, 68–74.

Baudrillard, Jean. *America.* Translated by Chris Turner. New York: Verso, 1988.

———. *Cool Memories IV: 1995–2000.* Translated by Chris Turner. New York: Verso, 2003.

Baumgarten, Marjorie. "Sitting in a Tin Can, Where Hell Is Still Other People: Director Duncan Jones on His Debut Film, 'Moon.'" *The Chronicle,* July 10, 2009. https://www.austinchronicle.com/screens/2009-07-10/808103/.

Beck, Don, and Christopher Cowan. *Spiral Dynamics: Mastering Values, Leadership, and Change.* New York: Wiley-Blackwell, 1996.

Bennett, J. "Q&A with Justin Broadrick." *Decibel Magazine,* January 2011, 40–42.

Berardi, Franco "Bifo." *Heroes: Mass Murder and Suicide.* New York: Verso, 2015.

Beste, Peter. *True Norwegian Black Metal: We Turn in the Night Consumed by Fire.* New York: Vice Books, 2008.

Boehme, Johannes. "An Interview with Rem Koolhaas." *The Believer,* January 31, 2020. https://culture.org/an-interview-with-rem-koolhaas/.

Bolton, Lucy. "'Under the Skin' and the Affective Alien Body." Paper presented at *Film-Philosophy Conference 2014: A World of Cinemas.* University of Glasgow, UK, January 2, 2014.

Bradbury, Ray. *The Illustrated Man.* New York: Doubleday, 1951.

———. *The Martian Chronicles.* New York: Doubleday, 1950.

Bradshaw, Peter, Deyan Sudjic, Dave Simpson, Iain Sinclair, and Mark Lawson. "How J.G. Ballard Cast His Shadow Right Across the Arts." *The Guardian,* April 20, 2009.

https://www.theguardian.com/books/2009/apr/20/jg-ballard-film-music-architecture-tv.

Braidotti, Rosi. *Nomadic Subjects: Embodiment and Sexual Difference in Contemporary Feminist Theory.* New York: Columbia University Press, 1994.

———. *The Posthuman.* Cambridge: Polity, 2013.

Bratton, Benjamin. *The Stack: On Software and Sovereignty.* Cambridge: MIT Press, 2015.

Brown, David Jay. "From Here to Alterity and Beyond with John C. Lilly." In *Mavericks of the Mind: Conversations for the New Millennium,* edited by David Jay Brown and Rebecca McClen Novick, 203–25. Berkeley: The Crossing Press, 1993.

Brown, Norman O. *Life Against Death: The Psychoanalytical Meaning of History.* Middletown: Wesleyan University Press, 1959.

Brummett, Barry. *Contemporary Apocalyptic Rhetoric.* New York: Praeger, 1991.

Burke, Kenneth. *Language as Symbolic Action: Essays on Life, Literature, and Method.* Berkeley: University of California Press, 1966.

Burnett, Joseph. "Extreme Language: An Interview with Justin K. Broadrick." *The Quietus,* May 9, 2012. http://thequietus.com/articles/08733-jk-flesh-interview-justin-broadrick.

Butler, Judith. *Gender Trouble: Feminism and the Subversion of Identity.* New York: Routledge, 1990.

———. *Precarious Life: The Powers of Mourning and Violence.* New York: Verso, 2004.

Calia, Michael. "Writer Nic Pizzolatto on Thomas Ligotti and the Weird Secrets of 'True Detective.'" *Wall Street Journal,* February 2, 2014. https://www.wsj.com/articles/BL-SEB-79577.

Card, Claudia. *The Atrocity Paradigm: A Theory of Evil.* New York: Oxford University Press, 2002.

Chang, Alvin. "Every Mass Shooting in the US – A Visual Database." *The Guardian,* June 2022. https://www.

theguardian.com/us-news/ng-interactive/2021/may/27/us-mass-shootings-database.

Chayefsky, Paddy. *Altered States: A Novel.* New York: HarperCollins, 1978.

Christopher, Roy. "Godflesh: Heads Ain't Ready." *SLAP Skateboard Magazine,* December 1997, 77.

———. "Godflesh: Uneasy Listening." *Pandemonium! Magazine,* October 1996, 22–23.

Clark, Andy. *Natural Born Cyborgs: Minds, Technologies, and the Future of Human Intelligence.* New York: Oxford University Press, 2003.

Clarke, George L. *Westlake and Selected Writings.* Los Angeles: Sargent House, 2017.

Clover, Carol J. *Men, Women, and Chain Saws: Gender in the Modern Horror Film.* Princeton: Princeton University Press, 1992.

Condon, Edward. *Final Report of the Scientific Study of Unidentified Flying Objects.* New York: Dutton, 1969.

Connole, Edia. "Seven Propositions on the Secret Kissing of 333 Black Metal: OSKVLVM." In *Mors Mystica: Black Metal Theory Symposium,* edited by Edia Connole and Nicola Masciandaro. London: Schism, 2015.

Connor, Steven. *Dumbstruck: A Cultural History of Ventriloquism.* Oxford: Oxford University Press, 2000.

Copenhaver, Brian R., trans. *Corpus Hermeticum.* Cambridge: Cambridge University Press, 1992.

Coupland, Douglas. *Generation X: Tales for An Accelerated Culture.* New York: St. Martin's Press, 1991.

Crane, Leah. "Elon Musk Demonstrated a Neuralink Brain Implant in a Live Pig." *NewScientist,* August 29, 2020. https://www.newscientist.com/article/2253274-elon-musk-demonstrated-a-neuralink-brain-implant-in-a-live-pig/.

Cronin, Claire. *Blue Light of the Screen: On Horror, Ghosts, and God.* London: Repeater Books, 2020.

Cross, Roger. *The Yorkshire Ripper: The In-Depth Study of a Mass Killer and his Methods.* London: HarperCollins UK, 1981.

Davis, Erik. *High Weirdness: Drugs, Esoterica, and Visionary Experience in the Seventies.* London: Strange Attractor, 2019.

———. *Techgnosis: Myth, Magic, and Mysticism in the Age of Information.* New York: Harmony, 1998.

———. "Terrence McKenna's Last Trip." *WIRED,* May 1, 2000. https://www.wired.com/2000/05/mckenna/.

Davis, Susan E., and Margo Demello. *Stories Rabbits Tell: A Natural and Cultural History of a Misunderstood Creature.* New York: Lantern Books, 2003.

de Certeau, Michel. *The Practice of Everyday Life.* Berkeley: University of California Press, 1984.

Delgado, José M.R. *Physical Control of the Mind: Toward a Psychocivilized Society.* New York: Harper & Row, 1969.

Denzler, Brenda. *The Lure of the Edge: Scientific Passions, Religious Beliefs, and the Pursuit of UFOs.* Berkeley: University of California Press, 2001.

Dery, Mark. *Escape Velocity: Cyberculture at the End of the Century.* New York: Grove Press, 1996.

———. *The Pyrotechnic Insanitarium: American Culture on the Brink.* New York: Grove Press, 1999.

Dick, Philip K. *Flow My Tears, the Policeman Said.* New York: Doubleday, 1974.

Dolar, Mladen. *A Voice and Nothing More.* Cambridge: MIT Press, 2006.

Douglas, Mary. *Implicit Meanings: Essays in Anthropology.* London: Routledge & Keegan Paul, 1975.

———. *Natural Symbols: Explorations in Cosmology.* London: Barrie & Rockliff, 1970.

———. *Purity and Danger: An Analysis of the Concepts of Pollution and Taboo.* London: Routledge & Keegan Paul, 1966.

Dyens, Ollivier. *Metal and Flesh: The Evolution of Man: Technology Takes Over.* Translated by Evan J. Bibbee and Ollivier Dyens. Cambridge: MIT Press, 2001.

Ebert, Roger. "Review of 'Crash' (1997)." *RogerEbert.com,* March 21, 1997. http://www.rogerebert.com/reviews/crash-1997.

Faber, Jonathan. *Under the Skin: A Novel.* New York: Harcourt, 2000.

Ferrante, Garth. "Godflesh Explains 'Selfless''s Song Titles." *Godflesh.com,* August 1994. https://godflesh.com/articles/int2.txt.

Fisher, Mark. *The Weird and the Eerie.* London: Repeater Books, 2016.

Fludd, Robert. "On the Occult and Wondrous Effects of Secret Music." In *Tractatus Apologeticus Integritatum Societatis de Rosea Crucis defendens.* Leiden, 1617.

Fuller, Curtis G. *Proceedings of the First International UFO Congress.* New York: Warner Books, 1980.

Galbraith, John Kenneth. *The New Industrial Society.* London: Hamish Hamilton, 1967.

Giannopoulos, Stavros. "Artist on Artist: Deafheaven." *B-Side,* July 4, 2015, B6–B7, B9.

Gibson, Andrew. *Misanthropy: The Critique of Humanity.* New York: Bloomsbury Academic, 2017.

Glaser, Anthony. "Interview: Deafheaven." *National Underground,* March 11, 2013. http://nationalunderground.org/2013/03/11/interview-deafheaven/.

Glenn, Jerome C., and Theodore J. *Futures Research Methodology, V2.0.* Washington, DC: AC/UNU Millennium Project, 2003.

Gorman, John. "Tanking." *OMNI Magazine,* August 1980, 61–64.

Gould, Stephen Jay. *Questioning the Millennium: A Rationalist's Guide to a Precisely Arbitrary Countdown.* New York: Crown, 1999.

Green, Ryan. *Trust Me: The True Story of Confession Killer Henry Lee Lucas.* Independently published, 2019.

Guffey, Robert. *Chameleo: A Strange but True Story of Invisible Spies, Heroin Addiction, and Homeland Security.* New York: O/R Books, 2015.

Gunn, Joshua. *Modern Occult Rhetoric: Mass Media and the Drama of Secrecy in the Twentieth Century.* Tuscaloosa: University of Alabama Press, 2005.

Hamilton Helle, Una, and Lotte Brown. *Becoming the Forest.* 3 vols. Antwerp: Het Bos, 2015–2019.

Haraway, Donna J. *Simians, Cyborgs, and Women: The Reinvention of Nature.* New York: Routledge, 1990.

Hayles, N. Katherine. *How We Became Posthuman: Virtual Bodies in Cybernetics, Literature, and Informatics.* Chicago: University of Chicago Press, 1999.

Hebdige, Dick. *Subculture: The Meaning of Style.* New York: Routledge, 1979.

Heikkilä, Melissa. "Machines Can Read Your Brain. There's Little That Can Stop Them." *Politico,* August 31, 2021. https://www.politico.eu/article/machines-brain-neurotechnology-neuroscience-privacy-neurorights-protection/.

Heim, Michael. *The Metaphysics of Virtual Reality.* Oxford: Oxford University Press, 1993.

———. *Virtual Realism.* Oxford: Oxford University Press, 1998.

Heller, Jason. "Deafheaven Profile." *Decibel Magazine,* August 2013, 32.

———. "Justin Broadrick of Jesu." *AV Club,* April 5, 2007. https://film.avclub.com/justin-broadrick-of-jesu-1798211103.

Hofstadter, Douglas. *Fluid Concepts and Creative Analogies: Computer Models of the Fundamental Mechanisms of Thought.* New York: Basic Books, 1995.

Hofstadter, Douglas, and Daniel C. Dennett. *The Mind's I: Fantasies and Reflections on Self and Soul.* New York: Bantam, 1981.

Hollinger, Veronica. "A History of the Future: Notes for an Archive." *Science Fiction Studies* 37, no. 1 (March 2010): 23–33. https://www.jstor.org/stable/40649583.

Hooper, Judith. "Interview: John Lilly." *OMNI Magazine,* January 1983, 57–58, 74–82.

Horsley, Jonathan. "Justin Broadrick Interview: Godflesh, Growing Up and Anarcho-Punk." *Decibel Magazine,* October 7, 2011. http://www.decibelmagazine.com/featured/justin-broadrick-interview-godflesh-growing-up-and-anarcho-punk/.

Howell, Linda. "The Cyborg Manifesto Revisited: Issues and Methods for Technocultural Feminism." In *Postmodern Apocalypse: Theory and Cultural Practice at the End,* edited by Richard Dellamora, 199–218. Philadelphia: University of Pennsylvania Press, 1995.

Howells, Tom. *Black Metal: Beyond the Darkness.* London: Black Dog Publishing, 2012.

Itzkoff, David. *Mad As Hell: The Making of Network and the Fateful Vision of the Angriest Man in Movies.* New York: Times Books, 2014.

Jansen, Karl. *Ketamine: Dreams and Realities.* San Jose: MAPS, 2001.

Jastrow, Robert. *The Enchanted Loom: Mind in the Universe.* New York: Simon & Schuster, 1984.

Johnson, Alex. "Between God and Flesh." *Thora-Zine* 9, 1995.

Jones, Barbara. *Voices from an Evil God: The True Story of the Yorkshire Ripper and the Woman Who Loved Him.* London: Blake Publishing, 1993.

Joy, Bill. "Why the Future Doesn't Need Us." *WIRED,* April 1, 2000. https://www.wired.com/2000/04/joy-2/.

Jouve, Nicole Ward. *"The Streetcleaner": The Yorkshire Ripper Case on Trial.* London: Marion Boyars, 1986.

Jung, Carl G. *Flying Saucers: A Modern Myth of Things Seen in the Skies.* Princeton: Princeton University Press, 1978.

———. *Man and His Symbols.* New York: Bantam, 1964.

Kelly, Richard. *The Donnie Darko Book.* London: Faber and Faber, 2003.

Kiang, Jessica. "'Crash': The Wreck of the Century." *The Criterion Collection,* December 1, 2020. https://www.criterion.com/current/posts/7206-crash-the-wreck-of-the-century.

Knapp, Bettina. *Machine, Metaphor, and the Writer: A Jungian View.* University Park: Pennsylvania University Press, 1989.

Koczan, J.J. "Jesu Interview: Justin Broadrick Confirms New Godflesh Studio Album, Discusses Jesu's Latest, Imperfection, Self-Indulgence, Roadburn, and Much

More." *The Obelisk,* May 6, 2011. http://theobelisk.net/
obelisk/2011/05/06/jesuinterview/.

Koestler, Arthur. *The Roots of Coincidence: An Excursion into
Parapsychology.* New York: Vintage, 1972.

Kraus, Chris. *Video Green: Los Angeles Art and the Triumph of
Nothingness.* New York: Semiotext(e), 2004.

Kroker, Arthur. *Body Drift: Butler, Hayles, Haraway.*
Minneapolis: University of Minnesota Press, 2012.

Kurzweil, Ray, "A Review of 'Her' by Ray Kurzweil." *Kurzweil,*
February 10, 2014. https://www.kurzweilai.net/a-review-of-
her-by-ray-kurzweil.

Lacan, Jacques. "Some Reflections on the Ego." *The
International Journal of Psychoanalysis* 34 (1953): 11–17.

Lakoff, George. "The Contemporary Theory of Metaphor." In
Metaphor and Thought, edited by Andrew Ortony, 202–51.
Cambridge: Cambridge University Press, 1993.

Langman, Peter, ed. "Eric Harris's Journal." *School Shooters
.info,* October 3, 2014. https://schoolshooters.info/sites/
default/files/harris_journal_1.3.pdf.

Lanier, Jaron. *You Are Not a Gadget: A Manifesto.* New York:
Alfred A. Knopf, 2010.

Lawrence, D.H. *Women in Love.* New York: Thomas Seltzer,
1920.

Lepselter, Susan. *The Resonance of Unseen Things: Poetics,
Power, Captivity, and UFOs in the American Uncanny.* Ann
Arbor: University of Michigan Press, 2016.

Leslie, Charles. "Review of *The Ritual Process: Structure and
Anti-Structure* by Victor W. Turner." *Science* 168, no. 3932
(May 1970): 702–4. DOI: 10.1126/science.168.3932.702.

Ligotti, Thomas. *The Conspiracy Against the Human Race.* New
York: Hippocampus Press, 2010.

Lilly, John C. *Programming and Metaprogramming in the
Human Biocomputer: Theory and Experiments.* New York:
The Julian Press, 1974.

———. *Simulations of God: The Science of Belief.* New York:
Simon and Schuster, 1975.

———. *The Center of the Cyclone: An Autobiography of Inner Space.* New York: The Julian Press, 1972.

———. *The Deep Self: Profound Relaxation and the Tank Isolation Technique.* New York: Simon and Schuster, 1977.

———. *The Scientist: A Novel Autobiography.* New York: Lippincott, 1978.

Lilly, John C., and E.J. Gold. *Tanks for the Memories: Floatation Tank Talks.* Penn Valley: Gateways Books & Tapes, 1996.

Lilly, John C., and Philip Hansen Bailey Lilly. *The Quiet Center.* Berkeley: Ronin Publishing, 2003.

Lockley, R.M. *The Private Life of the Rabbit.* New York: Macmillan Publishing, 1964.

Logan, William Bryant. *Dirt: The Ecstatic Skin of the Earth.* New York: Riverhead, 1995.

Lukes, Daniel. "Black Metal Machine: Theorizing Industrial Black Metal." In *Helvete: A Journal of Black Metal Theory, Issue 1,* edited by Amelia Ishmael, Zareen Price, Aspasia Stephanou, and Ben Woodard, 69–93. Brooklyn: punctum books, 2013.

Masciandaro, Nicola. "On the Mystical Love of Black Metal." In *Floating Tomb: Black Metal Theory,* edited by Nicola Masciandaro and Edia Connole, 101–14. Milan: Mimesis, 2015.

Maslin, Janet. "Screen: Ken Russell's 'Altered States.'" *The New York Times,* December 25, 1980. https://www.nytimes.com/1980/12/25/arts/screen-ken-russells-altered-states.html.

Mayakovsky, Vladimir. "A Cloud in Trousers." In *Russian Poetry: The Modern Period,* edited by John Glad and Daniel Weissbort. Iowa City: University of Iowa Press, 1978.

McLean, Adam. "Quantum Consciousness." *Alchemy Web Site.* https://www.alchemywebsite.com/quantum.html.

McLuhan, Marshall. *The Gutenberg Galaxy: The Making of Typographic Man.* Toronto: University of Toronto Press, 1962.

———. *Understanding Media: The Extensions of Man.* New York: Houghton-Mifflin, 1964.

Melton, J. Gordon. "The Contactees: A Survey." In *The Gods Have Landed: New Religions from Other Worlds,* edited by James R. Lewis, 1–13. Albany: University of New York Press, 1995.

Metzner, Ralph. "John Lilly and Ketamine: Some Personal Recollections." In *The Ketamine Papers: Science, Therapy, and Transformation,* edited by Phil Wolfson and Glenn Hertelius, 47–50. San Jose: Multidisciplinary Association for Psychedelic Studies, 2016.

Michael, Chris. "Spike Jonze on Letting 'Her' Rip and 'Being John Malkovich'." *The Guardian,* September 9, 2013. https://www.theguardian.com/film/filmblog/2013/sep/09/spike-jonze-her-scarlett-johansson.

Miéville, China. "Introduction." In J.G. Ballard, *Miracles of Life: Shanghai to Shepperton, An Autobiography*, ix–xiv. New York: Liveright, 2008.

Minsky, Marvin. "Telepresence." *OMNI Magazine,* June 1980, 45–52.

Moravec, Hans. *Mind Children: The Future of Robot and Human Intelligence*. Cambridge: Harvard University Press, 1988.

———. *Natural Symbols: Explorations in Cosmology.* London: Barrie & Rockliff, 1970. "The Senses Have No Future." In *The Virtual Dimension: Architecture, Representation, and Crash Culture,* edited by John Beckmann, 84–95. New York: Princeton Architectural Press, 1998.

Morton, Timothy. "At the Edge of the Smoking Pool of Death: Wolves in the Throne Room." In *Helvete: A Journal of Black Metal Theory Theory, Issue 1,* edited by Amelia Ishmael, Zareen Price, Aspasia Stephanou, and Ben Woodard, 21–28. Brooklyn: punctum books, 2013.

———. *Dark Ecology: For a Logic of Future Coexistence.* New York: Columbia University Press, 2016.

———. *Ecology without Nature: Rethinking Environmental Aesthetics.* Cambridge: Harvard University Press, 2010.

Moten, Fred. *Black and Blur: Consent Not to Be a Single Being.* Durham: Duke University Press, 2017.

Moyer, Matthew. "Wolves in the Throne Room: From Mount Olympia." *Ghettoblaster Magazine* 30 (Winter 2011).

Moynihan, Michael, and Didrik Søderlind. *Lords of Chaos: The Rise of the Satanic Metal Underground.* Port Townsend: Feral House, 1998.

Moynihan, Thomas. *X-Risk: How Humanity Discovered Its Own Extinction.* Falmouth: Urbanomic, 2020.

Mudrian, Albert. *Choosing Death: The Improbable History of Death Metal and Grindcore.* Port Townsend: Feral House, 2004.

Mudrian, Albert. "Godflesh's Justin Broadrick: 'I Never Feel Comfortable at Any Festival.'" *Decibel Magazine,* October 17, 2018. https://www.decibelmagazine.com/2018/10/17/godfleshs-justin-broadrick-i-never-feel-comfortable-at-any-festival/.

———. "Just Words from the Editor." *Decibel Magazine,* March 2007, 8.

Nash, Elle. *Nudes.* Ann Arbor: Short Flight/Long Drive Books, 2020.

Nasrallah, Dimitri. "Justin Broadrick: Napalm Death – Godflesh – Techno Animal – Jesu – Pale Sketcher." *Exclaim!,* September 2010. http://exclaim.ca/Features/Timeline/JUSTIN_BROADRICK-Napalm_Death-Godflesh-Techno_Animal-Jesu-Pale_Sketcher.

Noakes, Tim. "Under the Skin of Scarlett Johansson." *Dazed & Confused,* March 12, 2014. https://www.dazeddigital.com/artsandculture/article/19057/1/under-the-skin-of-scarlett-johansson.

Norris, Dr. Joel. *Henry Lee Lucas: The Shocking True Story of America's Most Notorious Serial Killer.* New York: Zebra, 1991.

O'Hehir, Andrew. Review "Sympathy for the Devil Worshipers: 'Until the Light Takes Us' Movie Review." *Salon,* December 7, 2009. https://www.salon.com/2009/12/07/until_the_light/

Parikka, Jussi. "Planetary Memories: After Extinction, the Imagined Future." In *After Extinction,* edited by Richard Grusin, 27–49. Minneapolis: University of Minnesota Press, 2018.

Parks, Andrew. "Wolves in the Throne Room Profile." *Decibel Magazine,* April 2009, 20.

Pasquinelli, Matteo. A*nimal Spirits: A Bestiary of the Commons.* Rotterdam: NAi Publishers, 2008.

Pasulka, Diana Walsh. *American Cosmic: UFOs, Religion, Technology.* Oxford: Oxford University Press, 2019.

Patterson, Dayal. *Black Metal: Into the Abyss.* London: Cult Never Dies, 2016.

———. *Black Metal: Prelude to the Cult.* London: Cult Never Dies, 2016.

———. *Black Metal: The Cult Never Dies, Volume One.* London: Cult Never Dies, 2015.

———. *Black Metal: The Evolution of the Cult.* Port Townsend: Feral House, 2013.

———. *The Cult Never Dies MegaZine.* London: Cult Never Dies, 2016.

Peak, David. "Nothing Will Have Happened: Speculation and Horror in the Anthropocene." In T*hinking Horror, Volume Two,* edited by S.J. Bagley, 198–206. Middletown: Thinking Horror, 2021.

———. *The Spectacle of the Void.* London: Schism, 2014.

Penny, Simon. *Making Sense: Cognition, Computing, Art, and Embodiment.* Cambridge: MIT Press, 2017.

Pessaro, Fred. "Big Ups: Deafheaven Pick Their Bandcamp Favorites." *Bandcamp Daily,* December 3, 2020. https://daily.bandcamp.com/big-ups/big-ups-deafheaven.

Petersen, Aage. "The Philosophy of Niels Bohr." *Bulletin of the Atomic Scientists* 19, no. 7 (1963): 8–14. DOI: 10.1080/00963402.1963.11454520.

Pettman, Dominic. *After the Orgy: Toward a Politics of Exhaustion.* Albany: SUNY Press, 2002.

———. *Look at the Bunny: Totem, Taboo, Technology.* Winchester: Zero Books, 2013.

Philips, Olav. *The Secret Space Age.* Kempton: Adventures Unlimited Press, 2015.

Pilkington, Mark. "In the Province of the Mind." F*rieze,* June–August 2018. https://www.frieze.com/article/what-was-inspiration-paddy-chayefskys-hallucinatory-novel.

Poscic, Antonio. "Out Demons Out." *The Wire,* April 2022, 30–38.

Prince, Stephen. *Apocalypse Cinema.* New Brunswick: Rutgers University Press, 2021.

Randle, Kevin D. *A History of UFO Crashes.* New York: Avon Books, 1995.

Raunig, Gerald. *A Thousand Machines: A Concise Philosophy of the Machine as Social Movement.* Translated by Aileen Derieg. New York: Semiotext(e), 2010.

———. *Dividuum: Machinic Capitalism and Molecular Revolution.* New York: Semiotext(e), 2016.

Realcaptainparsnips. "Their Bodies, Ourselves: Bodysnatching and the Male Gaze in 'Under the Skin.'" *Groupthink,* March 29, 2014. https://web.archive.org/web/20150222031724/http://groupthink.jezebel.com/their-bodies-ourselves-bodysnatching-and-the-male-gaz-1554476256.

Renfro, William L. *Issues Management in Strategic Planning.* Westport: Quorum Books, 1993.

Reuter, Jerome. "Stalaggh/Gulaggh: A Window into Suffering and the Necessity for Transgressive Art." *Diabolique Magazine,* November 15, 2020. https://diaboliquemagazine.com/stalaggh-gulaggh-a-window-into-suffering-and-the-necessity-for-transgressive-art/.

Reynolds, Simon. "Godflesh Streetcleaner." *Melody Maker,* October 14, 1989, 37.

Rice, David Leo. "The Overlook Hotel." *The Believer,* October 31, 2017. https://believermag.net/logger/overlook/.

Riches, Simon, ed. *The Philosophy of David Cronenberg.* Lexington: University Press of Kentucky, 2012.

Riesman, Abraham. "William Gibson Has a Theory About Our Cultural Obsession with Dystopias." *Vulture,* August

1, 2017. https://www.vulture.com/2017/08/william-gibson-archangel-apocalypses-dystopias.html.

Roberts, Adam. *It's the End of the World, But What Are We Really Afraid Of?* London: Elliott & Thompson Limited, 2020.

Roberts, Adam. *Science Fiction: The New Critical Idiom.* New York: Routledge, 2006.

Rotman, Brian. *Becoming Beside Ourselves: The Alphabet, Ghosts, and Distributed Human Being.* Durham: Duke University Press, 2008.

Rubin, Peter. *Future Presence: How Virtual Reality is Changing Human Connection, Intimacy, and the Limits of Ordinary Life.* New York: HarperOne, 2018.

Rucker, Rudy. "Outer Banks & New York #1." *Rudy's Blog,* August 2, 2015. http://www.rudyrucker.com/blog/2015/08/02/outer-banks-new-york-1/.

Rucker, Rudy. *Software: A Novel.* New York: Ace books, 1982.

Sager, Mike. "Fact: Five Out of Five Kids Who Murder Love Slayer." In *Revenge of the Donut Boys: True Stories of Lust, Fame, Survival, and Multiple Personality,* 103–20. New York: Thunder's Mouth Press, 2007.

Schneider, Kirk J. *Horror and the Holy: Wisdom-Teachings of the Monster Tale.* Chicago: Open Court, 1993.

SCI-Arc Channel. "Bruce Sterling & Benjamin Bratton in Conversation." *YouTube,* November 5, 2018. https://www.youtube.com/watch?v=Zo__x5SG8WY.

Sellars, Simon. *Applied Ballardianism: Memoir from a Parallel Universe.* Falmouth: Urbanomic, 2018.

———. "Learning to Live with Aggressionless Cars." *Foreground,* April 15, 2021. https://www.foreground.com.au/transport/learning-to-live-with-aggressionless-cars/.

Selzer, Jonathan. Liner Notes. On *Streetcleaner* [LP]. New York: Earache, 2010.

Serowy, Ulrike. *Skogtatt: A Novella.* Lohmar: Hablizel, 2013.

Shakespeare, Steven. "The Light That Illuminates Itself, The Dark That Soils Itself: Blackened Notes from Schelling's Underground." In *Hideous Gnosis: Black Metal Theory*

Symposium 1, edited by Nicola Masciandaro, 5–22. Lexington: CreateSpace, 2012.

Shanahan, Murray. *Embodiment and the Inner Life: Cognition and Consciousness in the Space of Possible Minds.* Oxford: Oxford University Press, 2010.

Shaviro, Steven. *Doom Patrols: A Theoretical Fiction about Postmodernism.* New York: Serpent's Tail, 1996.

———. *Post-Cinematic Affect.* Winchester: Zero Books, 2010.

———. "Swimming Pool." *The Pinocchio Theory,* January 29, 2004. http://www.shaviro.com/Blog/?m=200401.

Sherlock, Ben. "Long Live the New Flesh: 10 Behind the Scenes Facts about 'Videodrome.'" *Screen Rant,* August 1, 2020. https://screenrant.com/videodrome-movie-behind-scenes-facts/.

Shipley, Gary J. "Monster at the End: Pessimism's Locked Rooms and Impossible Crimes." In *True Detection,* edited by Edia Connole, Paul J. Ennis, and Nicola Masciandaro, 1–27. London: Schism, 2014.

———. *Serial Kitsch: An Epic Poem.* London: Schism, 2017.

———. *Stratagem of the Corpse: Dying with Baudrillard, a Study of Sickness and Simulacra.* London: Anthem Press, 2020.

———. "Visceral Incredulity, or Serial Killing as Necessary Anathema." In *Serial Killing: A Philosophical Anthology,* edited by Edia Connole and Gary J. Shipley, 21–37. London: Schism, 2015.

Sinclair, Upton. *Mental Radio: Does It Work, and How?* Springfield: Charles C. Thomas, 1930.

Smith, Anthony. *The Body.* New York: Walker & Company, 1968.

Smith, Bradley. "Interview with Wolves in the Throne Room." *Nocturnal Cult,* 2006. http://www.nocturnalcult.com/WITTRint.htm.

Smith, Zadie. "Sex and Wheels: Zadie Smith on J.G. Ballard's 'Crash.'" *The Guardian,* July 4, 2014. https://www.

theguardian.com/books/2014/jul/04/zadie-smith-jg-ballard-crash.

Steinbeck, John. *Of Mice and Men: A Novel.* New York: Covici-Friede, 1937.

Steinke, Darcey. "Satan's Cheerleaders." *SPIN Magazine,* February 1996, 62–68

Stengers, Isabelle. *In Catastrophic Times: Resisting the Coming Barbarism.* Translated by Andrew Goffey. Ann Arbor: Open Humanities Press, 2015.

Stine, G. Harry. "The Bionic Brain." *OMNI Magazine,* July 1979, 84–86, 121–22.

Stosuy, Brandon. "Meaningful Leaning Mess." In *Hideous Gnosis: Black Metal Theory Symposium 1,* edited by Nicola Masciandaro, 143–56. Lexington, CreateSpace, 2012.

———. "Show No Mercy." *Pitchfork,* June 20, 2007. https://pitchfork.com/features/show-no-mercy/6633-show-no-mercy/.

Stone, Allucquère Rosanne (Sandy). "Will the Real Body Please Stand Up?" In *Reading Digital Culture,* edited by David Trend, 185–98. Malden: Blackwell, 2001.

Suarez, Gary. "Voidhead: Justin Broadrick on the End of Godflesh." *Consequence,* February 9, 2015. https://consequence.net/aux-out/voidhead-justin-broadrick-on-the-end-of-godflesh/.

Svendsen, Lars. *A Philosophy of Evil.* Champaign: Dalkey Archive, 2010.

Tew, David T. ed. *Ketamine: Use and Abuse.* New York: CRC Press, 2015.

Thacker, Eugene. *Cosmic Pessimism.* Minneapolis: Univocal Publishing, 2015.

———. *In the Dust of This Planet: Horror of Philosophy, Volume 1.* Winchester: Zero Books, 2011.

———. *Infinite Resignation.* London: Repeater Books, 2018.

———. "Sound of the Abyss." In *Melancology: Black Metal Theory and Ecology,* edited by Scott Wilson, 179–91. Winchester: Zero Books, 2014.

————. *Starry Speculative Corpse: Horror of Philosophy, Volume 2.* Winchester: Zero Books, 2015.

————. *Tentacles Longer Than Night: Horror of Philosophy, Volume 3.* Winchester: Zero Books, 2015.

"The Shedding of Our Borrowed Human Bodies May Be Required in Order To Take Up Our New Bodies Belonging to the Next World." *HeavensGate.com,* August 18, 1994. https://heavensgate.com/book/611.htm.

The Weirdnet. "Scariest Music in the World?" *BitChute,* November 1, 2017. https://www.bitchute.com/video/zhsk3HVz5btd/.

Turkle, Sherry. *Alone Together: Why We Expect More from Technology and Less from Each Other.* New York: Basic Books, 2011.

Turner, Luke. "Greymachine: Justin Broadrick and Aaron Turner United." *The Quietus,* November 18, 2009. http://thequietus.com/articles/03246-greymachine-justin-broadrick-and-aaron-turner-united.

Turner, Victor. *Dramas, Fields, and Metaphors: Symbolic Action in Human Society.* Ithaca: Cornell University Press, 1974.

————. *The Ritual Process: Structure and Anti-Structure.* Ithaca: Cornell University Press, 1969.

Valcic, Vuk. "Godflesh revisits 'Streetcleaner.'" *Rock-A-Rolla Magazine,* June–July 2020, 28–29.

Vale, V., and Andrea Juno, eds. *RE/Search #8/9: J.G. Ballard.* San Francisco: Re/Search Publications, 1984.

Viola, Bill. *Reasons for Knocking at an Empty House: Writings 1973–1994.* Cambridge: MIT Press, 1995.

Virilio, Paul. *The Art of the Motor.* Translated by Julie Rose. Minneapolis: University of Minnesota Press, 1995.

————. "The Museum of Accidents." Translated by Chris Turner. *International Journal of Baudrillard Studies* 3, no. 2 (2006). https://baudrillardstudies.ubishops.ca/the-museum-of-accidents/.

von Däniken, Erich. *Chariots of the Gods.* New York: Berkeley Books, 1999.

Vronsky, Peter. *Serial Killers: The Method and Madness of Monsters.* New York: Berkeley Publishing, 2004.

——. *Sons of Cain: A History of Serial Killers from the Stone Age to the Present.* New York: Berkeley Publishing, 2018.

Vroon, P.A. "Man-Machine Analogs and Theoretical Mainstreams in Psychology." In *Current Issues in Theoretical Psychology: Selected and Edited Proceedings of the Founding Conference of the International Society for Theoretical Psychology,* edited by W. J. Baker, M.E. Hyland, H. Van Rappard, and A.W. Staats, 393–414. Amsterdam: Elsevier, 1987.

Walczak, René. "Godflesh: Strength Through Purity." *Propaganda* 19 (Fall 1992): 40–41.

Wallace-Wells, David. *The Uninhabitable Earth: Life after Warming.* New York: Tom Duggan Books, 2019.

Wark, McKenzie. *Dispositions.* Cromer: Salt Publishing, 2002.

——. *Molecular Red: Theory for the Anthropocene.* New York: Verso, 2015.

Weisman, Alan. *The World without Us.* New York: St. Martin's Press, 2007.

Weizenbaum, Joseph. *Computer Power and Human Reason.* San Francisco: W.H. Freeman, 1976.

Wilden, Anthony. *System and Structure: Essays in Communication and Exchange.* New York: Tavistock, 1972.

Williams, Evan Calder. *Combined and Uneven Apocalypse: Luciferian Marxism.* Winchester: Zero Books, 2011.

——. "The Headless Horsemen of the Apocalypse." *Hideous Gnosis: Black Metal Theory Symposium 1,* edited by Nicola Masciandaro, 129–42. Lexington: CreateSpace, 2012.

Wilson, Robert Anton. *Down to Earth.* Vol. 2 of *Cosmic Trigger.* Las Vegas: New Falcon, 1991.

Wilson, Scott. *The Politics of Insects: David Cronenberg's Cinema of Confrontation.* New York: Continuum, 2011.

Wolf-Meyer, Matthew J. *Theory for the World to Come: Speculative Fiction and Apocalyptic Anthropology.* Minneapolis: University of Minnesota Press, 2019.

Wolfe, Cary. *What Is Posthumanism?* Minneapolis: University of Minnesota Press, 2009.

Woodard, Ben. *On an Ungrounded Earth: Towards a New Geophilosophy*. Brooklyn: punctum books, 2013.

———. "The Blackish Green of the Greenish Black, or, The Earth's Coruscating Darkness." *Glossator* 6 (2011): 73–87.

Woodgate, Derek, with Wayne R. Pethrick. *Future Frequencies*. Austin: Fringecore Publishing, 2004.

Zeller, Benjamin E. *Heaven's Gate: America's UFO Religion.* New York: NYU Press, 2014.

Made in the USA
Middletown, DE
20 October 2022

13142917R00093